SOVIET
UNION
2 0 0 0

SOVIET UNION 2000

REFORM OR REVOLUTION?

2 0 0 0

WALTER LAQUEUR

with

John Erickson
Paul A. Goble
Edward Luttwak
Gur Ofer
Arthur Waldron

ST. MARTIN'S PRESS   NEW YORK

Design by Glen M. Edelstein

Library of Congress Cataloging-in-Publication Data

Laqueur, Walter.
    Soviet Union 2000 : reform or revolution?
        p.   cm.
    ISBN 0-312-04425-9
    1. Soviet Union—Politics and government—1985– I. Title.
DK286.L37 1990 947.085'4—dc20 89-77845

First Edition
10 9 8 7 6 5 4 3 2 1

Contents

vi • Contents

Acknowledgments

SOME TWO THIRDS OF THIS STUDY, were supported and reviewed by the Department of Defense. DOD review does not imply endorsement of factual accuracy or opinion. I would like to thank Andrew Marshall, whose interest made this study possible, and Leon Sloss for having given valuable help with organizing it. I would also like to thank the following for their parts in preparing the manuscript: Christina Jordan, Dorothy Tomaszewski, Alison Hoffman, Carolyn Winn, Edward Horgan, Alina Zyszkowski, and Janusz Bugajski.

Prologue

POLITICAL PREDICTIONS ARE easiest to make when they are least
needed, at a time when the political barometer points to continuity. They become most difficult at a time of rapid and violent
change. For those putting safety and caution above everything
else, comment on the present situation in the Soviet Union is a
subject to be shunned; they will be well advised to be guided by
the injunction to be silent and safe. But they may have to be silent
for a long time.

Our preoccupation in this study is not with the fate of an
individual leader, or a group of leaders, but with general developments affecting Soviet society and the Soviet state in the coming
decade. Such a review has to discuss a variety of possibilities,
which may disappoint those in search of certainties. However,
since Soviet politics are no more predestined than those of other
countries, one cannot reasonably expect much more. If a man will
begin with certainties (as Francis Bacon once noted), he shall end
in doubts; if he starts with possibilities, he may end in probabilities.

There is general agreement that momentous events have taken place in Eastern Europe and the Soviet Union. The potential implications of the reform movement in the Soviet Union are far-reaching, the revelations of *glasnost* astounding. It caused a wave of euphoria, more, admittedly, in the West than in the East, where greater awareness prevailed of the enormous difficulties facing the reformers. It also caused the breakdown of the Soviet empire in Eastern Europe.

By early 1989, however, it became clear that the results widely expected in the early stages of *perestroika* were not forthcoming. Some blamed it on the policymakers for not having been radical enough; others, complained that there had been too much experimenting on too many fronts, that the old system had by no means been all bad and that it was wrong to try to introduce to the Soviet Union all kinds of political, social, and economic systems (such as the market and parliamentary democracy) that were ill-suited to its traditions, aspirations, and specific needs. Yet others argued that it had been illusory to expect palpable change within a few years and that it would take decades to reform the country. In the meantime a strong hand would be needed to steer the country through the coming storms.

The skeptics predicted that the regime was not reformable and that the attempts to tinker with it would be in vain, merely resulting in further decline or perhaps even sudden collapse. Others, in a more optimistic vein, believed that the cohesive forces and inner resources of the country should not be underrated. Despite temporary failures, political zigzags, and setbacks, there would be progress in the long run. In any case, there was no alternative but to try. The crisis had existed for decades but under the conditions prevailing before 1985 it had been unthinkable to admit that the state of affairs had been less than perfect and the future prospects less than brilliant. A more realistic assessment began to prevail only with *glasnost.*

In the West it was widely argued that the changes had come as a total surprise. Who would have assumed in 1985 that within three years there would be so much freedom of expression? There had been the belief in some Western circles that the Soviet regime was relatively stable and the population relatively content. Similarly, some observers of the East German scene had assumed right up to Honecker's downfall in October 1989 that the regime was not unpopular and that in view of its many achievements the leadership had no reason to fear for its political survival. Others had taken a less sanguine view of conditions in Eastern Europe, aware of the unfolding crisis even if not of its full extent. But even those who had noted the signs of crisis were unable to say with any confidence when change would come and how exactly it would manifest itself.

Today, the situation is even more complicated than before 1985. Account has to be taken of political polarization and social and national unrest which could not show itself before to the same extent. Consistency was the fruit of stagnation, today there is not the one nor the other. Before 1985 nothing seemed possible except the perpetuation of the status quo, today there is an almost endless variety of possibilities.

The present study addresses itself to the more likely of these possibilities. It is improbable that by the end of this decade the Soviet Union will be a welfare state on the Scandinavian model and a well-functioning parliamentary democracy. Yet a total breakdown is almost equally unlikely in the near future, for reasons discussed further on in greater detail. Sensationalist scenarios make for exciting reading, but the obvious, even the trivial, usually provide safer guidelines. In the real world various stabilizers and retarding factors exist; societies frequently undergo crises, even grave and dangerous crises. They seldom commit suicide.

The years 1987–1989 witnessed a growing widening—as between the blades of a pair of scissors—between the creative-spiritual-cultural sphere, that is to say *glasnost*, and the material-economic sphere, namely *perestroika*. While *glasnost* made substantial progress, *perestroika* did not, and no gifts of prophesy were needed to realize that this process would not continue indefinitely. Everyone agreed that the Soviet Union was heading toward a very difficult period, but there was no unanimity as to how it would face the coming adversities. There was general agreement among informed observers that the end of authoritarianism in the Soviet Union was not around the corner, as some in the West and East had claimed in the early days of euphoria. No one, however, could say with any assurance how far and for how long the political leadership would again move in the direction of strong-arm politics.

If it is impossible to predict how the Soviet Union will be ruled and what the mood of society will be next year, it is possible to comment with greater conviction about longer-run political and economic probabilities, whatever the fate of individual leaders may be in the years to come.

One example of such kind of prediction should suffice. It concerns Eugen Richter (1838–1906), who was the leader of the Liberals in the German parliament during the last quarter of the nineteenth century, the bane of Bismarck, and an expert on budgetary affairs. In 1891, he wrote a little book, a political fantasy, in which he discussed the consequences of the establishment of a government on orthodox Marxist lines on German soil.[1] It would result, Richter wrote, in a mass escape over the borders. First the pensioners would flee; no great loss to the state. They would be followed by many artists and writers, but this too would not greatly disconcert the authorities because there would be enough writers left to sing the praises of the regime. Many intellectuals, in any case, were destructive elements and no obstacle should be put in their way. But then the exodus of skilled workers would follow—of engineers, teachers, and physicians. At this stage emigration would be stopped and the greatly strengthened border units would get orders to shoot to kill.

This was exactly what happened in East Germany. The question arises how anyone writing ninety-nine years earlier could have possibly foreseen the course of events. Eugen Richter was not a political philosopher of note nor a political science fiction writer

---

[1] *Sozialdemokratische Zukunftsbilder.* An English edition appeared in London a few years later.

of the rank of an H.G. Wells or a George Orwell. Rather, he was a man of common sense and knew instinctively that unless people had a minimum of freedom they would be unhappy, and if so, many would eventually try to escape. One of the great writers of antiquity wrote that common sense is the best prophet. It is not an infallible approach, but it is more often true than not, and there is so far no other method remotely as reliable.

Nineteen eighty-nine was an *annus mirabilis* in Eastern Europe. First Poland and Hungary, later on East Germany and Czechoslovakia, moved to radical reform as the traditional Communist power structures collapsed. It was an end of an era and it was enthusiastically welcomed by the overwhelming majority of the population. Furthermore, it proceeded without bloodshed except in Rumania. But it was also clear that the collapse of the dictatorships was merely the beginning of a difficult process of transition. All the countries of Eastern Europe confronted economic difficulties, for which there were no early and easy solutions in sight. Furthermore, democratic traditions in Eastern Europe were either feeble or had been suppressed for generations. While the ruling Communist parties had become universally unpopular, there was no certainty that the new democratic forces would show sufficient cohesion and determination, and that they would collaborate to safeguard a new order.

Above all, developments in Eastern Europe did not point the way to future trends in the Soviet Union, just as developments in the Soviet Union did not provide a clue to China. Communism is more deeply rooted in the Soviet Union than in Eastern Europe, it is no foreign importation. Russian nationalist opposition to Communism in the Soviet Union is not anti-imperialist, as is nationalist opposition in Eastern Europe. There is but little resistance against introducing a multi-party system and against private initiative in the economic sphere in Eastern Europe, but strong opposition against the market in the Soviet Union with the exception of the Baltic republics.

Thus the Soviet Union and Eastern Europe have moved in different directions and this has contributed to the general uncertainties. As the Brezhnev doctrine was abolished, the countries of Eastern Europe received much greater freedom to shape their own destiny. But it could still be taken for granted that there would be spheres of influence as long as there are big powers and small. Even at a time of internal crisis the Soviet leadership is unlikely to give up its predominant position in Eastern Europe. Neutrality is within reach for some Eastern European countries, but not affiliation with an alliance of which the Soviet Union disapproved. The Warsaw Pact may disappear, or, more likely perhaps, lose its importance, especially if NATO is reduced in scale and function. This leaves the question of German unity. The Soviet Union will accept a unified Germany but without enthusiasm and only on the basis of far-reaching guarantees.

The emergence of a united Germany will open new foreign political opportunities for the Soviet Union in a new European order. On one hand it is bound to lead, at the very least, to a weakening of NATO. On the other, the Soviet Union will be in demand in both Eastern and Western Europe as a counterweight to a united Germany. The new balance of power may well lead to realignments thought impossible only yesterday. Nor can it be excluded that if the major European countries will opt for social democracy in the 1990s and if there should be a similar trend inside the Soviet Union (an assumption that can by no means be taken for granted) the idea of the "Common European Home" or, at the very least, a new "Concert of Europe" may become more than a slogan.

Some Soviet commentators have argued that it has been so difficult to carry out reforms in their country because the seriousness of the situation was not generally realized, but that real change is bound to come once it is accepted that the nation is on the edge of an abyss. What kind of change do they have in mind? Not a few spokesmen have argued that there has been too much experimentation already and that only a return to the old system when everything was centrally planned (or at any case seemed to be centrally planned; the reality was often different) provided a way out of the dead end. Others have maintained that while the idea of the market and private initiative is repulsive to many Soviet citizens, it is still possible that a Soviet de Gaulle (a right-wing leader adopting left-wing measures) could persuade his countrymen to move forward. But the Soviet Union in 1990 is not France when the war in Algeria seemed to threaten the very existence of the republic. Just as the Russian Revolution, Stalin-ism, and the post-Stalin era were unique, comparison with other political regimes and societies are now only of limited help in providing clues, as the Communist system no longer works, and no alternative order has as yet emerged.

The rebellions in the non-Russian republics have come as a shock and as argued in the present study, the end is not yet near. But even the defection of some of them would not cause a deci-sive shift in the balance of power. It is not certain whether the seceding states would be viable. Even if the Soviet leadership were gradually to release, say Azerbaidjan, Lithuania, and Moldavia, it would affect only one or two percent of the area of the Soviet Union, less than five percent of the population, less than three percent of the oil production.

It is not likely that the non-Slav republics will secede from the Union within the next few years. There will be tension and conflict, at times probably violent. However, it seems far more probable that an attempt will be made to transform the present system into a looser confederation (or alternatively to impose unity by force). These efforts may succeed in some instances and fail in others. If they fail, the separatists are bound to gain the upper hand and the new Russia will consist of the present RSFSR in federation with the Ukraine, White Russia, and probably a few other republics.

The old "unbreakable union of free republics" (to quote the Soviet national anthem) is unraveling in front of our eyes. But it is useful to recall from time to time that in 1917 Russia seemed on the verge of total disintegration, and that Germany in 1945 lost almost half of her territory. Yet within three decades both coun-tries were back among the main players in world politics. In the final analysis the question whether the Soviet Union (or Greater

Russia) will remain a world power will be decided in Moscow, in the Kuzbass, the Urals, and in Siberia, not in Baku, Fergana, or Kaunas.

But these are long-term perspectives. The 1990s will certainly be a decade of great turbulence with, possibly, sudden changes in the leadership. The combination of economic crisis and separatist trends is not conducive to gradual democratization. Having to choose between chaos and tyranny, the majority has usually opted for a strong leadership. A great deal of fear, confusion, and sullen resentment has accumulated over the years in many sections of the population, in Russia as much as among the nationalities. This could open the door to political demagoguery: Surely someone must bear the responsibility for all that has gone wrong? There is a growing demand for purveyors of stab-in-the-back theories as there was in Germany after World War I. Many saviors of the fatherland offer their services as the last decade of the century was rung in from the towers of the Kremlin. Neither pogroms nor a political-military coup to bring public disorder to an end can be ruled out.

A study such as the present ought to try to look, not only beyond Gorbachev's successors but also beyond the successors' successor, however speculative this endeavor. Communism, by and large, has failed, but what are the options open to Soviet leaders in the post-Communist phase? Personalities will change and also, quite probably, their doctrines, but the problems facing the Soviet Union will more or less remain the same. Communism as an economic system has not worked and dictatorship has been discredited. But the prospects for a quasi-capitalist economic system are no more brilliant than those of a parliamentary democracy. A Chinese solution will not work forever even in China, let alone in more developed countries. Perhaps the Polish experience in the 1980s—military dictatorship as an interlude—points to a possible scenario. It is impossible to put the clock back indefinitely in the Soviet Union. Neither neo-Leninism, nor a conservative populism, nor a variety of fascism hitherto untried, will work. But equally it seems impossible to make a radical break with the past, as long as the majority of the population is not ready for basic innovation. So the country will be swaying between various political and economic systems until it will have found the one most appropriate for its mood and needs. The following scenarios all seem possible and it is quite likely that more than one will be tried in the years to come.

1. The adoption of radical measures in the political and economic field by the leadership, the gradual introduction of a multi-party system of sorts, far-reaching concessions to the nationalities including the right of secession, a free hand to farmers in the countryside, basic changes in industry and trade. However, there may not be sufficient popular support for a policy of this kind, in particular inasmuch as the economy is concerned; large sections of the bureaucracy will certainly try to torpedo it.

The opposition against the Communist party apparatus as it manifests itself in elections, demonstrations, strikes, and so forth, has not much in common except resentment about the privileges enjoyed by the *nomenklatura;* frustration and anger about the low standard of living; insufficient supplies; and the general dismal state of affairs. Some of the leaders of this opposition are populists of the left, others of the right, yet others look to Western societies for inspiration. Some are Communists of sorts, others anti-Communists. But neither has a clear idea how to confront some of the most pressing problems. A multi-party system has in effect existed inside the Communist party since 1988–1989. This state of affairs could continue for a number of years, but sooner or later a split is likely to occur along the same lines (conservatives, reformists, radicals). The drift away from Leninism will continue, other parties will be social democratic or non-socialist. There may be regional and ethnic blocs as in the old czarist Duma; a peasant party; left-wing and right-wing ecologists; Siberia-firsters; and perhaps even single issue pressure groups, be it abstinence or anti-Semitism. In view of the absence of a democratic tradition and the likelihood that no Soviet government will be able to make substantial progress within the next few years, an anti-democratic backlash seems likely at some future date.

The difficulties facing most Eastern European countries during the transition to a multi-party system, and the sprouting of dozens of national and regional groups, are indicative of the trouble that will confront the Soviet Union in the years to come. Given the absence of a democratic tradition, the polarization of public opinion, and the worsening economic situation, the prospects of Western style democracy in the Soviet Union cannot, at present, be rated very high; the most that can be reasonably hoped for is a presidential regime with certain democratic features in which the powers of decision are still concentrated in the hands of the president, who works through the state bureaucracy.

2. The emergence of a new centrist leadership from among the Politburo, either a single leader or a collective leadership using slogans such as "no more experiments," "normalization," "confidence should be restored to the people." The new leaders will be middle-of-the-roaders, who could appear with equal ease as moderates or conservatives, always according to the circumstances. Their main desire is to gain time. Such neo-Brezhnevism could be at best a temporary expedient.

3. A military dictatorship under populist auspices such as "Workers and Peasants rule without the Communist party" with a committee of national salvation on top. The army commanders will have the support of sections of the party leadership and the KGB. But the army will appear as the central force because of its prestige, despite the setbacks in recent years. ("Only the army can save us from the brink of the abyss.")

However, any such scenario rests on two preconditions which cannot necessarily be taken for granted: the unity of the army command, and the willingness of the soldiers to shoot, if given orders, on fellow Soviet citizens. Even if the army should be initially united in its readiness to act, subsequent disputes among the military leadership, coups, and countercoups, cannot be ruled out. The suppression of popular unrest by force of arms is a dangerous weapon. Once orders are not obeyed the whole edifice collapses; there is no longer a military option, only the threat of civil war.

4. Several variations can be envisaged on the basis of a military dictatorship scenario. By necessity it would be Russian-nationalist and populist. It could cling to as much of the empire as possible. Or it could opt for a Greater Russian solution letting the ingrate nationalities leave the Union, provided guarantees for Soviet security interests are given. The weakness of this scenario is that a regime of this kind has no answer to the basic economic and social problems besetting the Soviet Union. On D day plus one apathy would return, within a short time the country would be worse off than before.

5. A Kemalist, developmental, dictatorship aiming at leading the country gradually to democratic institutions and basic economic change by means of a revolution from above. This is similar in perspective to the first scenario. However, many Soviet observers believe that it is too late for a solution of this kind, which might have stood good chances during the years after Stalin's death.

6. Other developments such as the sudden emergence of a charismatic leader are always possible but less likely. Power at the center is sufficiently strong for the time being to suppress a civil war. But this is based on the assumption that the general disintegration will not go much further. If the center is further weakened, if the shortages, the general decay, the loss of confidence should go on, a civil war or more likely an old-fashioned Russian *bunt* becomes a possibility. A *bunt* is a popular revolt, destructive, essentially anarchic, lacking any clear aim, an explosion of the pent-up anger. But even a civil war or a *bunt* will not last forever, sooner or later centripetal forces will assert themselves, and out of the purgatory a new Russia might emerge.

It seems most likely that eventually the reform initiatives undertaken in 1986–1989 will be resumed, more thoroughly, more clearly thought out, and more radically. But no one can say for certain how long the detours may last and how much damage might be caused in between.

The most popular and talked-about figure in the Soviet Union, but also the most controversial, as the year 1989 drew to its close, was neither Mr. Gorbachev nor one of his opponents, but a certain Dr. Kashpirovsky. This television personality claimed in his frequent appearances to cure by hypnosis drug addiction and alcoholism and make intolerable pain decrease in intensity or disappear altogether. Many millions accepted his claims; most physicians and many others were unconvinced. But the Kashpirovsky phenomenon preoccupied public opinion like no other; there is a strong tradition of belief in miracle cures in Russia, stronger perhaps than in other parts of the world.

How strong is the belief in a political and economic Kashpirovsky cure—quick, radical, and above all painless? Long and bitter experience should have taught the Soviet people that there are no miracle cures in politics and even less in the economy; a healthy skepticism is indeed ingrained among the people. On the other hand, wide sections of the population have been exposed to disorientation for a long time. The graver the situation, the greater the temptation to follow false prophets. In the years to come much will depend upon the maturity of Soviet citizens facing adversity. And it is precisely at this point, with psychological rather than "objective" factors likely to decide the outcome of the struggle, that it becomes most difficult to predict it.

Walter Laqueur
March 1990

SOVIET
UNION
2000

•1•
SOVIET POLITICS: CURRENT TRENDS
Walter Laqueur

The Future of the Soviet Union: An Appraisal

HOW WIDE is the range of possibilities, as far as the direction is concerned, in which the Soviet Union will be moving in the years to come? Accident plays a role, and so do personalities. As the author of a letter published in a Soviet weekly recently noted, "The election of Gorbachev as general secretary of the party in 1985 was not foreordained, someone else might have been appointed, and in this case there would have been neither *glasnost* nor *perestroika.*" There is no denying this logic, but it is also true that the Soviet Union in 1985 faced a crisis—economic, social, and political. Any successor to Konstantin Chernenko would have been under strong pressure to tackle the problems confronting the country. In fact, Yuri Andropov, albeit in a halfhearted way, engaged in a reform course more preoccupied with *perestroika* than with *glasnost.* It is possible that a different style might have prevailed after 1985, that the demand for change might have

1

been more muted, that cultural freedom might have been far more restricted, and that the revelations might have been less extensive in scope. Perhaps Leonid Brezhnev and the period of *zastoi* (stagnation) would have been less roundly condemned. But it is unlikely that in the longer run—that is to say, over a period of five or ten years—any incumbent could have ignored the dangers confronting the Soviet economy and society, such as the deterioration in the mood of the public, the turn from relative optimism in the 1960s to pessimism, cynicism, and the decline in faith among the population.

But is it not possible that another leader might have pressed different policies to cope with the difficulties besetting the Soviet Union—say, a more aggressive line in foreign affairs, with greater emphasis on what is now euphemistically known as the "administrative-bureaucratic-command style"? Perhaps modernization and democratization would have figured less prominently in the propaganda, which would have followed traditional lines. It is not at all impossible that there will be a change in this direction, should present policies fail. But in 1985 the political barometer was pointing toward greater change. Continuation of the old and discredited policy would have aggravated the crisis, morale would have further declined, and the distance between Soviet reality and the official make-believe would have grown even further. There would not have been demonstrations in the streets of Moscow, Erevan and Tallin, but the process of decomposition from within would have continued, and the general putrefaction would have made a more severe crisis at some future date even more likely. An escape into foreign policy activism would not have helped. Afghanistan could have been subdued following the dispatch of more troops, but what would have been gained?

There was no willingness to accept the risk of a major war. By 1983 it had become obvious that the Soviet foreign policy of the previous decade had yielded meager returns: it had involved the country in an arms race it could ill afford, it had caused its potential enemies to rally, and in the Third World Soviet interests had not fared very well. True, a policy clearly aiming at further expansion, with all the costs and risks involved, might have appeared to be a real alternative to the prevailing state of affairs. But there was not much support for a hard line among either the leadership or the people.

Seen in retrospect, the election of Gorbachev was a historical accident, and it is doubtful that those who backed him were fully aware that their candidate would eventually press change further than they wanted. It is also true, seen in retrospect, that the Gorbachev alternative was the most likely response to the failure of earlier policies. There was no certainty that a reform policy would succeed, but it had to be tried.

Those who try to assess Soviet affairs today face a paradox: Far more information is available on many aspects of Soviet politics than has been for the last sixty years. Yet, while assessing the future of the Soviet Union has certainly become intellectually more challenging, it has certainly not become more simple. The pattern of Soviet conduct was overall more consistent and predictable under Stalin and his successors than it is today. New social and political forces have emerged (and are emerging) that make decision making more complex and more confusing. While the monopoly of political power of the party has in no way been broken and, if necessary, still will be applied without hesitation, there are now differences of opinion and interest on many aspects of Soviet domestic, economic, and foreign policy. It is not premature to talk about a deep and lasting division in the Soviet leadership. But these leaders are still tied together in many ways and will put up a common front against outsiders. If they are split, they are divided in more than two ways with regard to ideological orientation, style of leadership, enthusiasm for social and economic innovation, and their general priorities.

All of this means greater complexity: If under Stalin the will (or the caprice) of the dictator was the decisive factor, if under Nikita Khrushchev and Brezhnev differences in the leadership existed but were limited in scope, this is no longer so today. Nor is it likely to change in the foreseeable future. The general trend is toward division rather than unity, but division need not lead necessarily toward mortal conflict. It is a new experience for the Soviet Union to solve differences of opinion by debate and mutual concession, and there is no certainty that the experiment will succeed.

Over the centuries Russia has known long periods of tyranny and only a few months of freedom. The fact that serfdom was abolished only one hundred thirty years ago has deeply influenced mental attitudes and institutions. The Russian poet Mikhail Lermontov referred to a "country of masters and serfs . . . ," but contemporary Russia is no longer the Russia of 1860. A modern society cannot be run like an old Russian village, even though for some present-day nostalgic citizens this appears to be a matter of lasting regret.

The sociologist and philosopher Raymond Aron once wrote that revolutions occasionally succeed in France, but reforms never do. If Russian history were the only yardstick, Gorbachev's reforms, limited as they are, would seem to be doomed from the outset; the past teaches that the country needs a strong power to impose will and discipline. History also teaches that Russia has been an expanding power since the times of Dmitri Donskoi and Ivan Kalita. Change in Russia, with a few exceptions, always has come from above. Can freedom and independence, even in small rations, be imposed from above? Even if Gorbachev's reforms fail, they may take the country a few uncertain steps forward. Would it not be more correct to conclude that, while reforms never proved to be a full success in Russia, they did frequently bring about some change, from Peter the Great to Alexander II and Peter Stolypin?

There have been other nations (and religions) that followed a policy of militant expansion. All eventually reached their limit, because those who were threatened offered effective resistance, or because the expansive impetus weakened for a variety of reasons. One of the peculiarities of the age of *glasnost* has been a tendency to rethink the limits of the national interest and in some instances to cut the losses. This is not to say that Soviet isolationism seems a foregone conclusion at the present time, even though the Communist cause, which once seemed the wave of the future, has run out of steam; the idea of world revolution was dropped de facto many decades ago. The concept of forcibly imported revolution is no longer fashionable in any quarter of Soviet society.[1] The Soviet leadership may still seize geopolitical opportunities in various parts of the world, especially in proximity to Soviet borders (for instance, a power vacuum in Europe or the Middle East). But this has little to do with the specific ideological component that once made Soviet foreign policy different from the policy of all other powers.

Mention has been made of the difficulties that face those who try to assess future developments inside the Soviet Union. The number of factors involved has increased, and this adds complication even though these factors are better known than before. In any examination the extreme, most unlikely possibilities should be dismissed. Extreme possibilities include a full, speedy success for the Gorbachev reforms resulting in a dramatic economic and political improvement of the status quo of the Soviet Union within the next few years. Another extremely unlikely possibility is total failure, an internal breakdown resulting in the disintegration of the Soviet state. Once these possibilities are ignored, the range of those that remain is no longer impossibly wide.

What kind of change does the reform party envisage? Above all, innovation in the economic field and change in the political and social sphere insofar as the status quo impedes economic progress. Concentration on the economic sphere can easily be criticized. But it should be born in mind that the economic problems seem more urgent and the popular demand for such action universal, whereas the demand for political reform is limited, by and large, to certain parts of the population. Previous would-be reformers from Alexei Kosygin to Andropov advocated a certain amount of decentralization (which was never carried out) and relied on appeals to work harder. Gorbachev's proposals,

---

[1] It is perhaps significant that even contemporary Russian right wingers have argued that the invasion of Afghanistan was in the best tradition of Leon Trotsky.

based on suggestions made in the early 1980s by reform-minded economists and sociologists such as Abel Aganbegyan and Tatyana Zaslavskaya, are more far reaching. They amount to an appeal to go back to the NEP (New Economic Policy), meaning the relaxation of controls practiced under Lenin after War Communism virtually had paralyzed the economy. The present leaders realize that the situation now differs in essential respects from conditions prevailing in 1920. But certain basic ideas seemed as true then as they do now: to give greater play to market forces and private initiative (cooperatives rather than state enterprises), to encourage semi-private farming, and to reduce the power of the dead hand of bureaucracy which over the years has proscribed action in minute detail and effectively killed the spirit of initiative and responsibility. "Better less but better" had been the title of one of Lenin's last articles. This slogan and the demand for quality control have become the new commandment of the hour. For decades quantity rather than quality was the aim of Soviet economy and this resulted in absurd consequences: The Soviet Union produced many times as many tractors and harvester combines as the United States, yet in the end it had to import grain from America. It produced 800 million shoes yearly, three times as much as the United States, yet the quality was such that the country faced an acute footwear crisis.

"A return to the NEP" was not, however, an ideal program. It had dubious connotations; a "NEP-man" in Soviet parlance is a cheat and an exploiter, a negative type. It was easy to point to Lenin quotations in favor of the NEP, but it is also true that Lenin regarded the NEP as a transient phenomenon only, and it is not at all clear what ultimate aim the contemporary reformers have in mind. True, the antibureaucratic campaign has been popular; all Soviet citizens have suffered from this plague. But the lack of the spirit of entrepreneurship quite apart, there still is widespread fear, sometimes openly voiced, that the new reforms will end (like the NEP) with the repression of those who do well under the new economic policy. What the party has given, Soviet citizens know only too well, it can take back.

How might the population be assured that this time such fears are misplaced? The new leadership confronts a population that has been educated to obey blindly and not to question the wisdom of its superiors. Until recently it was only natural that the masses should assume that change for the better would come as a result of decisions made by the supreme leadership, endowed since Lenin's time with quasi-magical powers. Yet the greatest optimists among the reformers and their advisers know that the achievement of substantial results will take ten to fifteen years and longer. It will involve sweat, blood, and tears, and in the meantime the reformers will be more politically vulnerable than before. Workers are asked to work harder for the same wages, and in many instances for even lower wages.

The great pride of the Soviet system has been job security: However inefficient a factory, however low labor productivity, however small the demand for its output, no Soviet worker faced the danger of redundancy and dismissal and the need to look for another job. Now suddenly the specter of unemployment has appeared at the same time as the likelihood that some citizens, as the result of the new economic policy, will grow richer. Such a trend conflicts with the traditional Russian longing for equality (and the tradition of envy and jealousy). In brief, the reform politicians have opened themselves up to charges of betraying the ideals of socialism or, at least, egalitarianism. They expect workers living in conditions far inferior to those in developed countries to be as productive as their Western colleagues. In the 1930s and again in the 1950s there were massive ideological indoctrination and promises that life would be better and easier in the near future. But such propaganda lost its effects over the years. Alternatively, a system of instant rewards was introduced, but only a few benefited from this. In the 1990s consumer goods have to be imported from the West, a risky undertaking for which hard currency is lacking; only loans and credits could be of some help.

The economy is no doubt the most acute challenge facing the reformers, but the core of the crisis is psychological, not economic. It is the pessimism, the disbelief, the naked materialism, and the cynicism that has pervaded wide sections of the population. This mood cannot be cured simply by introducing more liberal economic methods. Something akin to a cultural revolution is needed. The reformers of the 1990s have appealed to common sense and self-interest; whereas those who wanted change sixty years earlier invoked the idealism of youth, of which there was a considerable reservoir. In this respect, as well as in others, there is a basic difference between the 1920s and the 1990s. The reformers of the 1990s are sensible people who recognize the economic and social ills and needs of the country. But neither by training nor by character are they leaders who can generate the mass enthusiasm needed for a cultural revolution, for a basic change in mood and motivation. At most, they can create the preconditions to abolish some of the restrictions that have put so many obstacles in the way of initiative and development. They can only hope that somehow a new spirit of enterprise, absent for so long, will evolve.

Western Assessments of Soviet Politics: Some Lessons of the Past

Seen in retrospect, the performances of Western Sovietology have not been impressive during the 1970s and early 1980s, and the media coverage of Soviet affairs has been, by and large, even weaker. The comments of Western leaders, at least to the extent that they were made for the record, have not been more illuminating. Readers of Western newspapers, and also readers of the more specialized literature during this period, could not be aware of the depth of the general crisis in the Soviet Union. True, it was widely reported that the Soviet economy was facing major difficulties and that the rates of productivity and general output were declining. But, with few exceptions, the extent of the political and social ills and the general immobility were not recognized. The achievements of the regime, its stability, and its popularity were over-rated. The reasons for this failure can be briefly summarized:

1. Some of it stemmed from political bias, not so much from pro-Sovietism as from a basically critical attitude toward Western policies and an inclination toward equidistance. This was perhaps more widespread in the United States since the Vietnam War, but to a certain extent it was present also in other Western countries, especially Britain and West Germany, less so in France and Italy.

2. Academic studies have to be based on facts and figures, not on impressions and instinct. Most of the available facts and figures concerning the Soviet Union were those issued by Soviet government spokesmen and publications. Furthermore, Soviet studies is a highly politicized field, and many of those practicing it have felt self-conscious. They did not want to repeat what they regarded as mistakes of the Cold War. Extreme judgments were eschewed lest they be interpreted as the result of political prejudice.

3. Representatives of the Western media stationed in the Soviet Union faced, for well-known reasons, greater difficulties than those in most other countries. This began to change to a certain extent in the *glasnost* era, but until 1986 the level of political coverage was poor (always with some notable exceptions). Moreover, many Western journalists were not sufficiently prepared for their assignment inasmuch as their background knowledge of things Russian and Soviet and their linguistic competence were concerned.

However, even among those who more acutely understood the unfolding crisis, the emergence of a new-style leader such as Gorbachev and an approach such as *glasnost* were not expected. Thus, the events of 1986–1989 surprised both those who for a decade or two had painted a picture that was far too rosy and those who had been aware of the dismal state of affairs but had not considered that at a certain stage attempts would be made to introduce reforms and changes. That the state of affairs inside the Soviet Union had been misread for some considerable time led to a cautious attitude on the part of Western observers during the first two years of Gorbachev's tenure. This began to change only in early 1987, as the reform policy gathered momentum.

A review of Western attitudes since then could start with the negative approach found among some experts both in Western capitals and in the Soviet Union. Some have argued that *perestroika* and *glasnost* were simply parts of a giant disinformation strategy aimed at inducing the West to lower its guard. If this had been the main or exclusive aim of the Soviet reform policy, the game hardly would have been worth the candle. True, *glasnost* was stressed in the propaganda directed to foreign countries. But *Ogonyok* was no less revealing than *Moscow News* and other flagships of the reform policy, and the idea that *glasnost* was only for foreign consumption was too farfetched to be taken seriously.

A somewhat greater number of experts has claimed that *glasnost* and reforms in general were a phenomenon known in the Russian language as *pokazukha* (for show only) or, alternatively, that the aggravating situation in the Soviet Union had compelled the leadership to press for certain reforms not because they were democrats or liberals at heart or social democrats, but because there had been a danger that the Soviet system would break down and the economy come to a standstill. Furthermore, they argued that, if the attempts at modernizing the Soviet economy succeeded, the country would constitute a greater military and political threat ten or fifteen years from now and that it was therefore not in Western interest to help the Soviet leadership in their reform policy.

This line of argument was based on a number of correct assumptions but also on others that were dubious. It took for granted that the Soviet leadership still constituted a more or less monolithic bloc except for some minor, unimportant, tactical differences. However, all indications pointed to the conclusion that, while present day Soviet leaders share some basic beliefs (as did Stalin and Trotsky or Khrushchev and Mao Zedong), there are fundamental policy differences between them. Ignoring these differences makes it next to impossible to understand the internal tug of war in the Kremlin. The conservatives in the Soviet leadership were not in principle opposed to economic reform; they only wanted not to go too fast and too far, and they wanted a minimum of political reform to go with it. The more radical reformers were convinced that, as long as the state kept the "commanding heights" in the economy firmly under its control, there was no danger to the socialist character of the regime. They believed, furthermore, that without some political reform ("democratization") the population would not actively participate. In other words, stagnation would continue. The conservatives agreed that some greater initiative from below was needed, but they felt that this could be elicited through administrative control and ideological indoctrination from above.

Finally, the argument that the Soviet Union could become militarily stronger and thus more dangerous to the West as the result of *perestroika* took for granted what even the most optimistic observer in Moscow thought impossible, namely a full success of reform policies in the near future resulting in substantial, steady, balanced growth over the next few years. But even if *perestroika* were to be a striking success, it was by no means certain that this would result in a greater military danger to the West; some Western observers have made in recent years the opposite case, that the Soviet leadership might adopt a more aggressive line in foreign policy because of failure to improve the state of the economy and social conditions at home—an escape into foreign activism, or even adventurism, as the result of domestic failure.

Advocates of this interpretation tend to exaggerate the extent to which the West can either hamper or help economic developments inside the Soviet Union. Soviet economic needs, and those of its allies, are such that the Western powers could not provide an aid program that would make a significant difference even if they wanted to. Credits and loans to the tune of $5 to 6 billion could make trade with the Soviet Union easier. (Trade with most European countries has substantially declined over the last three to four years.) But it would have no decisive effect on Soviet economic performance which, in any case, would not improve as the result of greater investment alone. The story of Soviet agriculture is a striking example of enormous investment resulting in few, if any, returns.

More influential among Western observers has been the opposite school of thought, which has tended to view the reform policy with a great deal of optimism. By and large it was believed in these circles that the reform policy constitutes a momentous turning point in Soviet politics, a second Russian revolution. Some analysts are more optimistic than others (economists are markedly less so than students of politics) with regard to a radical improvement. But the belief is widely shared that Gorbachev's attempts to democratize Soviet society are sincere and that most achievements, in any case, are irreversible; there will be no return to Brezhnevism, let alone to Stalinism.

Comments made by analysts belonging to this school of thought range from the acceptance at face value of official Soviet speeches and articles to a more sophisticated analysis of political and social trends inside the country. Thus it is argued that, while Soviet politics have remained rigid, Soviet society has undergone a veritable revolution over the last twenty years and that this is bound to result in far-reaching political change, sooner rather than later. It is undisputable that Soviet society is now quite different than it was under Stalin: The great majority of the population lives in cities, and a far greater percentage has higher education. Fifty years ago society was passive and willing to accept and carry out unquestioningly orders from above, but society today is more critical, has higher expectations, and has developed a momentum and orientations of its own. Such a society cannot be regimented in the traditional way, for it has its own ideas about running the country and wants a share in it.

These views are voiced frequently, and not only by analysts who are friendly toward the basic principles of socialism. The demographic changes that have taken place are real and value-free; the new generations coming to the fore in the Soviet Union are not necessarily better democrats, as some Westerners have argued. But they are certainly different in outlook, and they frequently oppose their elders and the establishment. This manifests itself sometimes in outrageous quasi-Fascist slogans or exploits or, more frequently, in a retreat from politics into something akin to a Soviet counterculture.

The socio-demographic interpretation is correct as far as it goes. The Soviet Union is not a country of illiterate *muzhiks* any more; in fact, it has not been one for decades. It seems plausible to conclude that a society consisting of many educated people cannot be run through institutions molded in the Stalin era which have changed since then only to a very limited extent. This refers not just to the recurrent purges and the "cult of the individual" so typical of the Stalin period which are regarded by many Soviet citizens in retrospect with horror and shame. It refers also to the fear and the passivity, the primitive propaganda and the intellectual regimentation which by no means vanished with the death of the dictator.

However, the assumption that higher living standards, urbanization, and more widespread education lead inevitably to democratic institutions has not been validated by historical experience. This assumption is based on a correlation between the GNP of a country and its level of freedom. But there is no historical law of this kind. The 14th-century Swiss peasants and Icelandic fishermen practiced democracy, even though their living standards were low by any standard, whereas 20th-century Germany's position among the most advanced industrialized countries did not prevent the rise of nazism. The contemporary Third World countries with the highest income are by no means the most democratic, and vice versa. Democracy is not merely a function of economic development, it is a state of mind based on political maturity, tolerance, self-discipline, and other attributes which have in some countries developed over generations, whereas elsewhere these qualities have remained underdeveloped.

We do not know why certain nations have shown a greater inclination and aptitude for democratic rule than have others, nor can it be argued that only a few nations are predestined to live in freedom and that democracy cannot be learned. However, experience has shown that nations become democratic only over long periods and that the imposition of democratic institutions (and constitutions) from above is usually of little avail unless basic democratic attitudes have developed among the population.

Russia has known some form of freedom (mixed with anarchy) for only a few months in her history; even if one adds to this the years of constitutional rule (1905–1907), it still is only a short time. The origins of the democratic movement in Russian political life go back a long time, but its fate has not been a happy one. This does not mean that democratization in Russia is forever doomed, but will be, in all probability, a protracted process. Among the obstacles is an antidemocratic vested interest, the powerful bureaucracy. The aspirations of substantial sections of the population have not been fulfilled through democracy; the coincidence of nationalist tensions with political and social ferment is not conducive to the growth of freedom. Mention already has been made of an antidemocratic ideology that argues that history shows that Russians find it difficult to live with a surfeit of freedom and that without a strong ruler the country may fall apart. It also ought to be recalled that many democratic reformers of the 1990s do not by any means aim at a pluralistic, parliamentary, Western-style democracy but rather at something more modest: They want a one-party state with laws guaranteeing elementary freedoms to the individual citizen.

However, in the absence of true democratic choice such guarantees cannot be securely anchored; they will depend on the goodwill and the enlightened spirit of a self-perpetuating governing stratum. Such a political system will be no more than a halfway house between dictatorship and democracy. While social trends can favor or impede the progress toward democracy, they do not prescribe the character of the political system. Urbanization solves certain problems but creates many others, and the claims made by some Western social scientists postulating steady and more or less certain progress toward democracy have been excessive.

Other Western observers have expressed optimism, for a variety of reasons, about the outcome of the reforms initiated by Gorbachev. Some claim that the reforms are bound to succeed despite temporary setbacks, simply because there are no alternatives. The conservatives and the neo-Stalinists (they argue) have had their day, and they have failed. They have no concrete program to cope with the difficulties confronting the country, which, in large part, are the result of their past policies or, at least, their inability to recognize problems and deal with them in good time. However, history teaches that there are always political alternatives; the fact that the conservatives have not succeeded in the past may result in a temporary political setback for them. But it still could be true that their basic ideas are closer to the mood of the country, which opposes experimentation and change. In that case the reform policy will be no more than an interlude, especially if it should appear after a number of years that the reformers have not been more successful than their predecessors have been in coping with the basic problems facing the country.

One approach that has not been discussed so far could be defined as "realistic." This viewpoint does not suggest that success or failure of the reform policies is foreordained. It takes into account Russian experience, but it is also aware that discontinuities occur and that, while the past offers valuable clues for the future, it contains no guarantee that future developments will always follow past patterns. A realistic approach considers subjective as well as objective factors, the competence, farsightedness, idealism, or the lack of these qualities among leaders and masses as well as demographic, social, and economic trends. It takes into account ideology in the widest sense: cultural traditions, nationalism, and religion. It tries to identify the main factors and actors that will influence developments in the years to come. It cannot predict the role of individual leaders, which may be decisive.

Many examples can be found in modern history of predictions that came true despite being based on entirely wrong assumptions: As the course of events is not predestined, there can be no guarantees for correct predictions. Nonetheless, some approaches to assess future trends are more reliable than others, and the only guidance at our disposal is provided by past experience and rational analysis.

A Note on Russian Predictions

The history of Soviet political predictions since 1917 remains to be written and analyzed. Many émigrés expected the immediate downfall of Soviet power (called *Sovdepia* in those circles in the early days). Inside the Soviet Union, especially after the end of the civil war and the consolidation of Bolshevik power, the party expected that the revolution would prevail in the not-too-distant future all over the world; the building of socialism in one country was only a temporary expedient. As the Soviet Union grew stronger, "returners" among the émigrés and the "national Bolsheviks" predicted the early demise of Leninism, the strengthening of the traditional national elements, and the gradual normalization, as they saw it, of internal conditions. This school of thought had a renaissance between 1943–1946.

In recent times Andrei Amalric's *Will the Soviet Union Survive until 1984,* written in 1969, has been of special interest. The author correctly noted that the regime had lost its dynamism, and he stressed the growing stagnation along with the strengthening of nationalist ideas. He argued that the system had to introduce change in order to survive but was incapable of doing so. In this state of paralysis Amalric saw the danger of a violent explosion of anger from the dark masses, who felt threatened. He saw some hope in the emergence of a new middle class. In foreign policy he took for granted a protracted and destructive conflict between the U.S.S.R. and China.

Amalric's predictions sharply contrasted with those of other dissidents, such as Andrei Sakharov, who thought that reform was possible and who envisaged, at least for a time, a convergence between West and East, a concept that had been developed in the democratic countries in the early 1960s. Some émigrés, such as Alexander Solzhenitsyn, were much more pessimistic, and Alexander Zinoviev believed that the Stalinist order was effective and would last forever.

The Reform Party

By 1985 conviction was widespread that the direction of Soviet internal development had taken a wrong turn, that the economic state of affairs and social conditions had deteriorated. This conviction was shared by Russian patriots of the right and intellectual critics belonging to the democratic-liberal camp. The most powerful literary indictments came from the right; it is difficult to imagine more devastating accounts of the moral deterioration in society than Victor Astafiev's *Sad Detective* and Valentin Rasputin's *Fire*—the naked egoism, the moral degradation, the growth of crime and drunkenness, the crass materialism—there was hardly a ray of hope in these pitiless descriptions of life in Soviet villages and small towns. Other conservative sources indicated that life in the anonymous big cities was even worse.

The criticism of domestic affairs from the democratic forces did not come as a surprise, but even the patriotic element, usually so reluctant to admit any blemish, saw hardly a gleam of hope. The situation clearly had become critical. Sections of the leadership and their families were shielded from the hardships, shortages and indignities of daily life. They did not have to stand in lines for many hours to make essential purchases; they were living in something like a ghetto of their own with their own shops, hospitals, schools for their children, and personal transport. They met the masses through the windows of their chauffeured cars. There is a revealing scene in one of the post-1985 bestsellers (*New Appointment* by Alexander Bek) that describes how two government ministers whose cars do not turn up at the appointed time are at a total loss: Never having used public transport they do not know how to purchase a subway ticket.

True, there is every reason to believe that the organs of state security reported on the mood of the population, and it is probably no accident that Andropov was among the most reform-minded leaders of his time. But he was steeped in the Stalinist tradition. An elderly man in indifferent health when his turn came, he apparently could not envisage change by any means other than imposing stricter discipline from above. There is evidence that some of the truly farsighted and honest party leaders, both in the center and on the regional level, either had an intuitive feeling or knew through personal observation that a crisis had arisen. Some were uttering warnings privately, but they were not united, and they had no clear concept of how change could be implemented. Furthermore, the secrecy and the compartmentalization of the regime prevented even highly placed leaders from gaining a full, realistic picture of the extent and depth of the general decline. Thus, those who specialized in agriculture were, of course, fully aware of the low productivity, the general lack of initiative, the unnecessary losses, and the growing deficits from year to year despite increased subventions, but they still could harbor illusions that the state of affairs in other parts of the country and other sectors of the economy was much better, that their own experience was somehow atypical. The secrecy engulfing every part of Soviet society made it possible for whole sections of the country to move to a post-Communist age in which criminal gangs, while paying lip service to official ideology and paying tribute to the central leadership in more tangible ways, had established a mafia-like rule, keeping slave farms and cheating the state of billions of rubles which they pocketed, as in the case of the nonexistent cotton crops in Uzbekistan.

The population of the Soviet Union was materially better off in 1985 than it had been twenty years earlier, and there was less oppression than in 1955. Nevertheless, a spirit of relative optimism had turned, over those decades, into pessimism. The Russian people are not extravagant in their tastes, and while industrial and agricultural output grew (albeit slowly and fitfully in the 1950s and 1960s) foreign observers reached the conclusion that, since the standard of living had also increased, there was little acute unhappiness among the population. However, economic growth declined and then came to a virtual standstill in the late 1970s. Worse yet, the distance between official propaganda and the real state of affairs increased all the time. Before the Second World War it had been relatively easy to explain the shortcomings of the regime with reference to the need for forced industrialization. Later on, the war effort and the ravages of the war served to explain Soviet poverty and backwardness.

As the years passed, the memories of occupation receded into the background, and, as other countries that had suffered from the war recovered in unexpectedly short periods, the confidence of the people waned. True, there were still impressive achievements in space travel and in the buildup of military power, but in other respects the state of affairs in the Soviet Union began to resemble Third World conditions, while other countries forged ahead. The old explanations were no longer persuasive, and no new ones replaced them (except perhaps the need to build up the armed forces to "thwart the aggressive designs of the imperialists").

The official propaganda continued to refer to the Soviet Union as one of the world's richest countries, a society in which justice and freedom prevailed more than in any other. But no access to privileged information, no propaganda from foreign radio stations was needed to realize that this was simply not true; anyone with his or her eyes open realized that Soviet society was in a physical as well as moral decline and that new, energetic leadership was needed to get the country moving again. In other countries such initiative could have come from below, but not in the Soviet

Union. Furthermore, the channels of communications were blocked, as it was strictly illegal to talk or write openly about the true state of affairs. Reform in Russian history, from Peter I to the emancipation of the serfs and Stolypin's agrarian policy before World War I, had always come from above, usually against considerable resistance. As Alexander Pushkin once noted, "Our government are the only Westernizers. . . ."

The initiative could come only from inside the party, but where would such an initiative find support? A feeling of urgency, a conviction that change was imperative was needed, but public opinion in the Soviet Union existed only *in statu nascendi*. Ironically, the Bolshevik party had come to power under the slogan of the mobilization of the masses, yet for a long time past, the masses had been more or less systematically demobilized. Dissatisfaction among the workers and in the villages had manifested itself in drunkenness, rowdiness, and other negative ways. In the service sectors there were opportunities to engage in black market activities, and the intelligentsia had been inclined to seek personal fulfillment in the private rather than the public sphere of life. Nevertheless, once conditions deteriorated beyond a certain point, men and women in many walks of life appeared who supported a reform initiative even if they, for one reason or another, were not capable of acting as leaders or militants in the reform movement.

Most active in this respect was the technical intelligentsia, partly because they were more open to new ideas and better able to articulate them, and partly because many of them had a better idea of the extent of the problems facing the country than did the factory workers or the peasants. Thus the intelligentsia became the mainstay of the reform movement. As a result, some outside observers came to underrate the movement's potential importance. Of what consequence was a political movement that appealed mainly to a few intellectuals in the capital and perhaps in a few other big cities? But this misjudged both the quantitative extent and the qualitative role of the intelligentsia in the Soviet Union.

The intelligentsia is not limited to a few avant-garde writers, artists, and thinkers; it includes many millions of people. Even if not every one of them is an ardent fighter for *glasnost* and *perestroika,* their importance as a group of men and women of ideas, of communicators whose message through radio, television and the printed word reaches the last village, should not be underrated. The intelligentsia provided the ideology of the reformers, and it also helped Gorbachev in his attempts to persuade the people to make a major effort to tackle the main problems. Under the Soviet system the feeling had been deeply ingrained in the population that there was an almost impassable divide between "them" and "us"; politics was something ordered from above. The new reforms were based on the assumption that there also would be initiative, enterprise, and active participation from below, that the scope of activity of the state and party bureaucracy should be restricted. In this context *glasnost* seemed crucial; unless the people were told how serious the situation was, chances for active collaboration would be small.

On this point the leadership was divided from the very beginning. Some, such as Yegor Ligachev, thought that a little *glasnost* was desirable but that if it went too far the result would be counterproductive, and despair and more apathy would ensue. At the beginning, even Gorbachev was in favor of only very limited *glasnost,* never *glasnost* for *glasnost's* sake. Some of his supporters among the intelligentsia pressed the revelations considerably further than he had intended, and this caused a great deal of strife among the leaders as time went on. It is true that Gorbachev and his supporters in the party leadership were more radical fighters for *glasnost* in 1988 than they had been two years earlier, or at least they were willing to give a freer hand to the intellectuals who claimed that there would be no progress without at least some further democratization. However, the main interest of the party leadership, as it has been frequently emphasized, was in the economic field. How to increase productivity as well as the quality of the output was their main concern. Cultural liberalization was welcome as long as it did not go too far and proved to be not too divisive. New thinking in foreign policy was equally desirable, inasmuch as it improved the international standing of the Soviet Union and helped to repair the damage caused by the rigidity and the outdated concepts that had shaped Soviet foreign policy not only in the Stalin era but also during the years of stagnation.

There were distinct differences of opinion from the very beginning as to how far and how fast reform should go in various fields, and collisions were inevitable within the camp of reformers. One of the bones of contention was how to treat those who had belonged to the antireform camp prior to 1985 but had recognized their errors, or at least pretended to do so. Should their transgressions be forgiven, or should they be distrusted and kept at arms length? This was an important question, but there were many others of even greater importance, relating not so much to the past as to the future. They concerned, above all, the political future of the regime.

During 1989 polarization of public opinion became even more pronounced. The anti-reform forces rallied and were more outspoken than before. The reformers split: The establishment liberals, including Gorbachev, were pressing without much success for more rapid *perestroika* while putting a stop to further political liberalization. The radicals stressed that there would be no progress without speedy and far-reaching reform, that is to say breaking the political monopoly of the Communist party and introducing greater economic freedom in industry, agriculture, and the service sector.

Resistance to Change

Resistance to change comes from social groups that have a vested interest in the *status quo*, from people ideologically opposed to change, from those who fear it, and above all from the inertia that has existed for centuries in Russian society, which has been systematically inculcated for a long time.

The fear of freedom is a syndrome noted by psychologists in

various ages and parts of the world, and its sources have been studied for a long time. This has been noted by not a few Russians who have argued that the Russian political mind throughout history has shown less enthusiasm for *liberté* than for *fraternité* and *égalité*. But others have argued that there is not much room for *fraternité* in the absence of freedom. In the presence of a strong leader and a *nomenklatura, égalité* has frequently meant the demand that "nobody should live better than myself." Whatever the reasons, the longing for security is deeply ingrained in Soviet society. Hence the rejection of economic liberty with all its concomitant risks (failure, bankruptcy, unemployment). Hence the greater enthusiasm for the Japanese model in which, it is believed, the entrepreneur accepts responsibility for his employees in good times and bad.

Much of the criticism of the reformers has been directed against the bureaucracy, and there is no doubt that Soviet society is the most overadministered in the world. All party and state institutions have grown immensely over the decades. Before communism came to power Lenin predicted that bureaucracy would be overcome by proletarian consciousness: "All may become bureaucrats for a time and therefore nobody will be able to become a bureaucrat". He could not have been more mistaken, and by the time of his death he realized it. By 1924 the Soviet Council of National Economy had one controller for every productive employee. Whereas in Czarist Russia the country had been run by two dozen ministers, some eight hundred ministries and government committees with the rank of a ministry existed by 1985. The total number of bureaucrats was estimated at sixteen million, but it may have been larger still.

A cynic might argue that such gross overstaffing had its advantages. It prevented unemployment, for many of those shuffling papers were incapable of productive work in any case. But the existence of such a huge army of bureaucrats, had several important consequences. They had to justify their existence, and thus they introduced regulations that made every aspect of Soviet life more cumbersome, made change and indeed any initiative next to impossible. The main evil was not the number of nongainfully employed but their negative impact, from the leaders of the supreme state-planning authority, Gosplan, to the last local administrator. In a certain Soviet ministry, one employee's job was only to insure that maps of the country were kept under lock and key and that nobody had access to them; there were probably many thousands like him. The main damage to the national economy and to society was not from the salary paid to these guardians of state secrets, it was from the many man hours lost and the wrong decisions taken because essential information was kept from the Soviet public for no good reason. A quotation from the young Marx which no one had ever invoked previously became very popular in the *glasnost* years: Secrecy was the essential spirit of bureaucracy, and the observation of secrecy was safeguarded by its hierarchical character.[2]

It would be a mistake to conclude that all members of the bureaucracy oppose reform; this was not the case in Czarist Russia, and it is not true in the Soviet Union. Exceptions can be found above all in the higher echelons, where there is less reason to fear losing jobs or privileges than there is further down in the hierarchy. Furthermore, there are exceptions among those bureaucrats whose assignment is, broadly speaking, to get things done, in contrast to those whose function is to control or prevent, or those who have no clear assignment at all. The bureaucrats who have to deliver goods or services find themselves tied down by a system that complicates every transaction and creates unnecessary difficulties. They face the same difficulties as do leading technocrats or directors of factories or the heads of collective farms. Most scientists and technologists favor abolishing this system that prevents the free flow of information, both from abroad and internally, a system that does not reward achievement but rather rewards caution and inactivity. The scientific bureaucrats, on the other hand, will not easily give up a system that ensures their

---

[2]V. Rubanov, in *Kommunist*, 13, 1988, p. 27. Rubanov is introduced as the head of a department in a scientific research institute of the KGB.

control. Some of them may side with the reformist scientists, but most will not, for far-reaching changes flatly contradict the conservative spirit in which they have been trained. There is instinctive as well as ideological resistance against change. History has convinced the conservatives that change has been usually for the worse. The conservative camp includes heterogenous elements—neo-Stalinists on one hand, anti-Marxist Russian patriots on the other. The neo-Stalinists have no use for the Dostoyevskian mystique and the back-to-the-village romanticism of the Russia-firsters. The patriots, on the other hand, believe that the revolution of 1917, inspired by Marxism-Leninism, was an unmitigated disaster that did untold damage to Russian values and culture. They are willing to concede mitigating circumstances to Stalin because he destroyed the original Bolshevik party, with its strongly internationalist ethos, and also because he made Russia a strong military power.

The conservative camp covers a wide gamut of opinions, from enlightened patriotism to a lunatic fringe that sees everywhere the "hidden hand," conspiracies to undermine and subvert Russian values by means of Western (mainly American) mass culture, rock and roll, alcoholism, drugs, pornography, and other stratagems. The "hidden hand" is controlled by Freemasons, Jews and other "satanic forces," a catchall term encompassing everyone who happens to disagree with the extremists. The views of the more extreme elements are as important as those of the moderates, both because of the number of the militants and their fellow travellers and because of the support they enjoy in senior party circles, in the army, and also in some government departments.

While the conservatives basically do not disagree with the reformers' analysis of the social and economic ills of the country, they have no sympathy for the democratic reform program. They oppose self-management in industry; the neo-Stalinists among them are against even private plots and family brigades in agriculture. Above all, they are against market socialism, which they claim is a contradiction in terms. They firmly believe that a return to NEP-like conditions would benefit only a small section of the population, not society as a whole. Their economic program, which their critics have termed "national utopianism," is based on the tacit assumption that, while the situation is bad, it will not significantly improve in any case. Even a growth rate of 3 to 5 percent over a number of years would not bring about radical improvement in living standards. Hence, they conclude "We cannot compete with the Japanese, the West Europeans, and the Americans. But unlike them we have not sold our soul to mammon; we have other priorities and spiritual values, which our enemies lack."

The perception that most or all foreigners hate Russia is deeply rooted among members of this camp. They believe that Russophobia is not necessarily connected with anticommunism. The fact that it existed before 1917 and that it is still going strong now, even though communism is no longer a decisive issue, has convinced them that in the final analysis Russia has no friends and that in a state of emergency no one but Russians can be trusted. Given these assumptions, it is only logical not even to try to compete with the foreigners but rather to improve the situation by emphasizing order, discipline, and the political and moral indoctrination of the masses.

The weakness of this program is as evident as was the weakness of fascism. The dissatisfaction with the big city and the longing for a return to old-style village life are at odds with superpower ambitions, which imply a modern industry able to equip a powerful army. Patriotism in massive doses will not induce workers and peasants to work harder for any length of time, let alone to buy shoddy goods for the sole reason that they are "our own" goods. Furthermore, Russian nationalist extremism faces one handicap that fascism in Italy and Germany did not confront: Whereas Hitler and Mussolini could appeal to the patriotic beliefs of 98 percent of their countrymen, only half of the population of the Soviet Union is actually of Russian origin. The invocation of the great Russian heroes and victories of past ages will have no attraction for the other nationalities. In fact, such slogans are divisive and may well antagonize them.

The basic beliefs of the Russian right such as the anti-capitalist nostalgia are deeply rooted and based on resentment and unhappiness with the prevailing situation. They are not based on what Marxists call a "scientific analysis." There is not one economist of renown among them, and their program is based on the writings of amateurs.

The right wing has tried to take the initiative in combatting various social ills. They have been in the forefront of fighting alcoholism and of preserving old monuments, but they have done so with so much exaggeration and shrillness and the proclamation of so many falsehoods as to discredit the cause they want to promote and to encourage further splits in society. While the conservatives have the political and moral support of some widely read novelists and poets, the rank and file is petty bourgeois (in Western terms) with a sprinkling of the military and policemen.

Some Soviet social scientists, notably Igor Bestuzhev-Lada, have tried to define various categories of opponents of reform. He has noted a great deal of pro-Stalinist sentiment among the generation of the veterans of the Second World War. They believed in their leader, it is said that they went into battle shouting: "For our fatherland, for Stalin." (This has been disputed, however, by many contemporaries.) Surely their sacrifices and the death of so many of their friends and relations could not have been in vain? The 1930s, after all, was a time not only of mass executions but also of great industrial progress and constructive activities. Was it not true, as Stalin said in 1935, that "Comrades, life had become better?" These veterans view with dismay the young generation of the 1980s which, in contrast to the buoyant spirit of optimism and the readiness to sacrifice of their own youth, lacks idealism. Many members of the older generation oppose change, either out of inner conviction or because they have been effectively brainwashed. Others have far from positive memories of the Stalin era, because they, or those close to them, were subjected to repression. But it was still true that, among the older generation more than any other group, resentment has prevailed about the general trend of Soviet policy under Gorbachev. Since even the younger members of this group are in their sixties, though, it is only a question of time until they vanish.

Yet another group of veterans, much smaller in number but younger and more active, constitutes a potential reservoir for the opponents of reform: the soldiers who fought in Afghanistan. They are not opposed to political change per se, but, like German and Italian veterans of World War I, they have grievances against a society and government that has not fully recognized their efforts and sacrifices. They therefore have become easy prey to all kinds of extremist groups.

Another interesting distinction should be noted. Not all those who defend Stalinist practices are true believers. There is reason to believe that not a few are cynics who do not subscribe to Communist doctrine but who think that, given the political immaturity, essential lack of discipline, and inclination toward anarchism of the common people, an iron fist is needed to impose order. Their attitude reminds one of certain eighteenth- and nineteenth-century thinkers who ceased to believe in God but still believed that religion was "necessary for the common people."

The greatest number of those not joining the reform camp are not, however, actively opposed to it. These men and women are indifferent or apathetic, beyond the reach of the promises and threats of the official propaganda. They even might feel some sympathy for the aims of the reformers, but they have heard similar slogans too often in the past, and they think that in the end there will be no improvement. Others are tempted to cooperate, but they also know from experience or from the stories told by their parents that it is dangerous to show excessive enthusiasm. In the 1920s the peasants were told to grow rich, only to be arrested and exiled a few years later.

It is all very well to encourage people to speak freely, but perhaps it is only a trick by the authorities to find out the identity of the malcontents. Even if the authorities are totally sincere, there is no guarantee against another change in power in the near future and the reimposition of strict controls. In this case, those who have been too outspoken and daring under *glasnost* are bound to suffer. The antireformers have one great advantage over their foes: while change involves action, opposition does not involve any effort, and inaction is sufficient to bring about the failure of the new schemes. While some conservative spokesmen talked as early as 1987 about a "veritable civil war" (or a confrontation similar to Stalingrad) going on between the radical reformers and their opponents, this was an exaggeration. Open enmity toward reform is fairly rare and not very dangerous, from Gorbachev's point of view. The real threat is sabotage through inaction and through the general lethargy that has been symptomatic of Soviet society for a long time. It all boils down to whether the regime is at all amenable to basic change, except as the result of a major traumatic shock or over a long time.

The Limits of Glasnost

The cult of secrecy predates the revolution of 1917; foreign visitors from the sixteenth century agreed that Russian authorities did what they could to keep information from foreigners, and also from their own people. Russian government from an early date was based on *neglasnost*, known in Western intelligence parlance as the need-to-know principle. Before 1914, Russia was the only European country that made passports and visas mandatory, and its censorship, at least up to 1905, was more severe than it was in other countries. Yet, compared with the control and restrictions of the Stalinist era, Czarist Russia seems in retrospect almost a permissive society, and even after the relaxation of controls in the post-Stalin age censorship remained far more severe than it was before 1917. A telephone directory was a top-secret document, and detailed maps of Soviet cities did not exist or were deliberately falsified. In the words of the Soviet Union's chief cartographer, "Almost everything was changed on those maps. Roads and rivers were moved, city quarters turned around, streets and buildings wrongly indicated. On a tourist map of Moscow, for example, only the contours of the capital would be partly accurate." Vital statistics regularly published in all developed countries either were kept secret or were falsified. This pertained not just to information of conceivable military interest but to all information including, for instance, the suicide rate and the production of essential commodities.

Probably the most important achievement of *glasnost* was the demonopolization of information, which, however modest, amounted to the beginning of a veritable revolution in Soviet life. *Glasnost* was most thorough at the very top, that is to say in the capital and in the national media. As a Soviet observer put it, there was much less *glasnost* at the republican level, say in Kiev or Tashkent, and outside the bigger cities there was not much of it at all. Thus, to give an example, many revelations were made about the sad state of Soviet medicine, the low level of competence, the lack of essential drugs, even that free medical care was a mere fiction and that whoever wanted competent treatment and care had to pay for it. However, such admissions of shortcomings only seldomly trickled down. While the minister and the leading media would make all kinds of startling revelations, the individual hospital or regional medical center would only seldom follow suit.

Why *glasnost*? The partial opening-up of the Soviet system occurred not to please outside critics but because the all-pervasive secrecy caused more harm to the Soviet Union than it did to outsiders. It made economic as well as scientific-technological innovation difficult, and it greatly hampered economic and social planning. The revelations were not, of course, a total break with the past, for the condition of a country of almost 300 million inhabitants could not be kept totally secret, even if half of it was still out of bounds to foreigners. Many attentive visitors recognized well before Gorbachev that the country faced a major alcoholism problem, even though the full extent was not known. The same was true of other social evils. To give another example, novels and plays that conveyed an impression of widespread corruption had been published. Ecological debates had preceded *glasnost,* for instance the debate about the rerouting of Siberian rivers. Other topics, admittedly, were considered taboo. Even if the social evils could not be mentioned in print, on radio, and on television, millions knew that the general state of affairs was not good and that urgent problems were swept under the carpet, and there were open debates at least in small circles. But the general impression was that, although regrettable shortcomings existed, these were the exceptions rather than the rule, and they were being energetically tackled by those in power.

The difference with *glasnost* was that many suddenly realized that the opinions voiced previously only among trusted friends in fact were shared by a great many people. These opinions pertained to education, to the ecological balance, to agriculture and life in the countryside in general, to crime, drugs, abortion, and prostitution, to the many millions living below the poverty line, and to the state of affairs in Soviet literature, arts, the media, and even in many scientific disciplines. It was conceded that most social services functioned badly. Perhaps more significantly, it was admitted that the general mood of the country had soured. It appeared that many people had become hard, egoistical, cynical, and preoccupied with obtaining and maintaining material comforts. The idealism of former times had disappeared, and the cry of despair asked by a leading Russian novelist, Vasili Shukshin, in the early 1970s—"What has become of us?"—was suddenly in everyone's mouth: Why are the masses so sullen, so full of discontent?

In these and other fields a wide-ranging debate began, first in the central media and later on, in a more cautious way, outside Moscow. However, even under *glasnost* wide stretches of public life were only partly opened up for public debate, and other areas remained, by and large, part of the zone of silence. The grey zone included political debates and decision making at the top, the social differences between the ordinary citizen and the *nomenklatura*, and also the recent history of the Soviet Union.

All nations have stretches in their history of which they are not proud, but elsewhere determined attempts have been made to come to terms with the past. In the Soviet Union for decades after Stalin's death there was such a fear of telling the truth and confronting the Stalinist heritage that only a halfhearted attempt was made, under Khrushchev, to lift the curtain of silence. After Khrushchev's downfall, Stalin, not his victims, was rehabilitated. Since new generations had grown up in the meantime, the burden of the past might have become much lighter, but this was not the case. There had been, after all, many millions of victims, and there was no good reason that their children would forgive and forget. Perhaps even more important, the real issue was not the dead dictator but Stalinism, which in its institutionalized form has continued to pervade many walks of Soviet politics and society.

There was, at least among sections of the population, a genuine moral revulsion against the official mendacity that had prevailed for almost seven decades. As Yuri Afanasiev, a leading Soviet historian, said, "In no other country has history been so much falsified as in ours." But the forces against making a clean break with the past were strong, and not just because most historians have resisted any major revisions. A radical reexamination of Soviet history would establish that the overall balance of Soviet history at least since Lenin had been negative. This, of course, was a totally unacceptable conclusion for the party leadership. It would have fatally undermined the party's legitimacy. It would have called into question the theories of Lenin and Marx, the basic tenets of communism. Hence the warnings by members of the Politburo, including Gorbachev, not to go too far in reexamining the past.

The picture that emerged was carefully balanced, with the revelation of crimes and "deviations from the norm" on one hand, and the great socialist achievements on the other. The guardians of ideological purity warned that a "one-sided approach" would have incalculable consequences, undermining the faith of the masses in the party, in its leadership, and in communism in general.

Resentment against the privileges enjoyed by the *nomenklatura*, while fairly widespread, was at first not as acute as expected. Large sections of the population accepted that even under communism there would be wide differences in living standards and that, to a certain extent, the children of upper classes would inherit some privileges or at least get a head start. Complaints became more acute when supplies became shorter and lines longer. But although a frontal assault on privilege was sharply rejected in 1986–1987, measures were taken to make the system less conspicuous, to close down some of the shops catering only to the *nomenklatura*. This, no doubt, helped to defuse a potentially dangerous situation.

Far less tractable was the upsurge of nationalism that occurred under *glasnost*. Nationalist tensions had, of course, existed in equal measure before *glasnost*, only their outward manifestations had been suppressed. Furthermore, under Brezhnev a modified version of the Austro-Hungarian and Ottoman imperial system had been used. Leading representatives of the various minorities had been co-opted both at the top level and in the regions to share in running the system. These leaders were often dubious characters who openly practiced nepotism and corruption on a massive scale, particularly in Central Asia and Caucasia. However, within limits the system did work. The police and the various control institutions in Moscow were instructed to ignore the misdeeds of the local *mafiosi*. They kept order in their republics, and, while there was some resistance against this scandalous state of affairs, the local leaders easily silenced such criticism.

Furthermore, there was even greater leniency on the part of the local population; the local leaders were known to be scoundrels, but they were native scoundrels. The situation recalled the state of affairs in some Third World countries after decolonization: Foreign rulers would never have been forgiven for the sort of behavior practiced by the local elites that succeeded them. *Glasnost* began to change all of this. As the true state of affairs became known, attempts of reform were made, and these hurt the incumbents. The conviction grew in Moscow that in Central Asia the leadership could rely only on a very few local Communists.

The situation in the Caucasia and the Baltic republics was different. In Armenia the enmity was directed not so much against the Russians as against neighbors and age-old foes. Corruption had not been a major issue in the Baltic republics, but there was great resentment against Russian immigrants and great fear that the original inhabitants would be swamped by newcomers and lose their national identity. Russian immigration even was compared by some with the Chernobyl disaster. While living standards in Central Asia were lower than they were in Russia, they were markedly higher in the small Baltic republics, which complained about "colonial exploitation": They claimed that they paid Moscow but received nothing in return.

In the Ukraine, the second biggest of the Soviet republics and the one culturally and in other respects closest to Moscow, *glasnost* also brought much resentment to the surface. But it was less acute, and Moscow was more willing to make concessions. The local leadership was changed only belatedly and concessions were made to the Ukrainians in the cultural field.

Some sectors of public life were affected hardly at all by *glasnost.* The debates among the supreme party leadership were known only in rough outline. It was known that differences of opinion existed between Ligachev on one hand and Gorbachev and Alexander Yakovlev on the other; other Politburo members kept a low profile. But, unlike in the 1920s, the policy differences were not often discussed openly, they were only hinted at, and if Gorbachev was subjected from time to time to tough speaking by ordinary citizens this had mainly to do with the unsatisfactory state of food supplies rather than with specific policies. Equally, Ligachev was criticized by a few daring intellectuals for his authoritarian style and for the company he kept rather than for the policies he advocated, about which not enough was known.

Two other institutions were largely shielded from public scrutiny: the armed forces and the KGB. True, they too swore allegiance to *perestroika,* although there were not many reforms that outside observers could detect with the naked eye. Personnel changes took place among the army leadership, but these might have come in any case. As far as the state security organs were concerned there was a remarkable continuity in leadership;

changes were made, but they were in-house. The army was criticized for mistreatment and bullying of recruits *(dedovshchina)*, but complaints were directed not against the supreme command but against junior officers. From time to time the wisdom of Soviet strategy was questioned: Why were the SS 20s deployed, only to be scrapped later on? Why had the Soviet Union been drawn into an arms race it could ill afford?

This led to a debate about "sufficiency" as distinct from superiority, which had been the overall aim of Soviet strategists since the end of World War II. This debate pitted civilians against military strategists, and the former had the support of the country's political leadership, which was laboring under severe economic constraints. While the new military commanders stressed the need for reform and "new thinking," this referred more to the modernization of the army than to the modification of basic strategy.

There was little desire to accept massive cuts in defense spending, just as there was no great eagerness to make the details of the defense budget known. The military leadership participated in the political debates: "Pacifist" intellectuals were attacked, as was the lack of patriotism among sections of the younger generation. Some scientists had argued that requiring science students to serve in the armed forces during the most creative years of their lives had a detrimental influence on Soviet science, an argument that was strongly resented by army spokesmen. On the other hand, open support was given to the Russian nationalist groups that emerged in 1986–1989, both within the establishment and outside it. Furthermore, the political leadership was and would continue to be obliquely reminded from time to time that Khrushchev had been overthrown in part because he had lost the confidence of the army as a result of cuts in the military budget which made necessary the pensioning off of hundreds of thousands of officers.

The KGB seemed by and large to have been more reform minded than were the armed forces; it certainly had a better grasp of public relations. Through its operations abroad it had gained a better understanding of the relative weakness of the Soviet Union compared with other advanced industrialized countries. Through its domestic operations it had a more realistic picture of internal shortcomings. But the KGB had a collective, institutional desire not to give up any of its functions in society and politics. On the contrary, if the Soviet Union confronted so many difficulties and challenges at home and abroad, could it not be argued that state security was still of paramount importance? Whether a reorganization was advisable—whether, for instance, there should be an organizational division between operations at home and abroad—was in the final analysis a mere technical question. There is reason to assume that the KGB was instrumental in helping Gorbachev to be appointed and that it supported him during the first years of his incumbency. But the speeches of Victor Chebrikov in 1987 (still head of the KGB at the time) made it clear that *glasnost* had gone too far, that the intellectuals were too negative in their approach, and that the nationalities, unless kept under tight control, would cause major trouble.

Individual KGB officers came under fire for having exceeded or misused their power (for instance in the Ukraine), and some of them were demoted, but the institution itself was exempt from attack. It was always stressed that the KGB bore no responsibility for the crimes of the GPU and the NKVD, its predecessors in the 1930s and 1940s, nor did it perpetuate the cult of secrecy which pervaded all sections of Soviet society. Some efforts were made to emphasize the openness of the work of the KGB, but these were, by and large, halfhearted and amateurish attempts. The "revelations" sponsored by the KGB about its past exploits did not go beyond what had been known before, and in many cases they were untrue or misleading. If certain concessions were made to *glasnost* they were cosmetic or concerned unimportant issues. There were no far-reaching changes, nor could there be, given the character of the regime. The coexistence between *glasnost* and the organs of state security was bound to be uneasy. The decisive question was not whether or how far the KGB could be liberalized or democratized, but how important a political actor it was likely to be in the tug-of-war in the party leadership. The KGB for decades has been under strict control of the party leadership. But, if the party leadership is no longer united, there is at least the possibility that this could change.

·2·
SOVIET POLITICS: FUTURE SCENARIOS
Walter Laqueur

Prospects for Reform

TO WHAT EXTENT do the prospects of reform depend on the long-term success of the economic policies of the regime? Total economic failure resulting in declining living standards and acute shortages of food and other vital commodities would fatally weaken the regime. This would cause dissension within the party leadership and generate pressure for a change of policy, and also of the policymakers.

Such a possibility can by no means be excluded. But it seems more likely that economic policies will fail in some respects but show modest progress in others, that some sections of the population will benefit (or suffer) more than others. The political consequences of uneven economic development are, of course, much more difficult to predict. Success and failure in any case are relative factors, and they must be assessed in their historical, political, and psychological context. They must be compared with the economic performance of past periods in Soviet history, especially the most recent periods. They also must be compared with the economic situation in other parts of the world.

If the other developed industrial nations go through a period of substantial and uninterrupted prosperity, even skillful Soviet propaganda will face an uphill struggle to explain to the Soviet people the growing discrepancy between the poor economic performance of their own country and the brilliant success of the West and Japan. The essential facts about the functioning of the world economy and the economic state of other countries cannot be kept secret. Nor can they be explained away with reference to an allegedly higher quality of life and other nonmeasurable factors in the Soviet Union while there are growing complaints about the quality of life inside the Soviet Union. True, it has been argued for decades that the Soviet system has certain features that appeal to Soviet people more than capitalism, with its various ugly faces. These features include job security, absence of extremes of rich and poor, and well-functioning social services.

The longing for job security is very real, it is taken for granted, and it has become one of the major obstacles on the road to Soviet economic reform. For this reason the Japanese system, with its strong paternalistic features, appeals more to many Russians than does the American system, with its high degree of job insecurity. As for the absence of extremes of wealth and poverty it is indeed true that there are no billionaires in the Soviet Union, but enormous differences (by Soviet standards) still exist between the way of life of the average citizen and that of those in privileged positions. This has eroded much of the belief that there is much more social justice in the Soviet system. It also was long believed that capitalist countries did not have social services comparable to those of the Soviet Union. But for years knowledge has spread about the true state of affairs, and this too has had a negative effect on morale and on the legitimacy of the regime.

Economic success may be the most important single factor as far as the future of Gorbachevism is concerned. But it is by no means the only factor, nor will it be necessarily the decisive issue except, as has been said, in the case of total failure. There is no automatic nexus between economic performance and political success, no Micawberish law proclaiming that, say, a 4 percent annual growth rate spells happiness, whereas a lower growth rate inevitably results in misery. Perception, popular mood, and expectations also matter.

EXPECTATIONS

Soviet citizens have been told since the mid-1930s that life has improved and that they will be much happier yet in the near future. The slogan *"dognat i peregnat"* (to catch up and overtake) was coined in the 1930s. Under Khrushchev an official date was proclaimed for when America's overall production and standards of living would be overtaken. After 1945 the propaganda machine explained shortages and difficulties with reference to the ravages of the war. This seemed plausible enough at the time, but the more the memory of the war receded into the past, the less persuasive this argument became. How to explain that countries that also had been ravaged by the war forged ahead at far quicker speed than the Soviet Union? Thus the growing pessimism of the 1970s was largely a result of the impossibly high promises made by the Soviet leaders.

Other considerations were also involved: There had been, after all, economic progress in the 1950s and 1960s, and the new pessimism had as much to do with the realization that, despite the facts that so many new apartments had been built and that there was no longer hunger, there was no more happiness. And so it came to pass that one of the most popular songs of the 1930s, *"Shiroka strana moia rodnaia"* (from the film *Tsirk*), which said that there was no country in the world in which people were breathing as freely, became a frequently invoked butt of ridicule, a prime example of official hypocrisy. One could point to similar trends in the West, culminating in the youth revolt of 1968. But there was at least one basic difference: Western ideology (if indeed there was such a thing) had never made such extravagant promises. For Marxism-Leninism, on the other hand, the claim of outproducing the rest of the world was absolutely essential, and so was the corollary, that a rich society would also be a content society.

OPTIMISM AND PESSIMISM

Russian official ideology has always been optimistic. This was the case under the Czars and *a fortiori* during the Soviet period. It was perhaps most succinctly expressed in Stalin's famous speech in Moscow on April 13, 1928, "There are no fortresses in the world which the Bolsheviks cannot take." However, unlike in the United States, the official optimism was by no means shared by all sections of the population. There was little of it among the working class, except perhaps in the most highly paid sections, and hardly any among agricultural workers.

Russian pessimism, not only among the intelligentsia, has a long and interesting history. A wave of pessimism engulfed the country in the 1970s, resembling in some ways a similar mood around the turn of the century, when there had been much dejection despite substantial economic development.[1] It is not always easy to explain the change of a national mood with reference to objective factors, and sometimes it is altogether impossible. The case of France between the 1870s and 1914 is instructive: Almost everyone in France was convinced that the ultimate decline and fall of the nation was at hand. Observers explained that this was the result of the lost war against Germany, demographic decline, the rise of alcoholism, and many other negative trends in French society. Yet after 1905 the mood suddenly changed, even though the demographic decline, alcoholism, quality of political leadership, and other objective factors remained constant.

The change in mood of a nation may be connected with gener-

---

[1] Annual industrial growth in Russia between 1885 and 1914 was 5.7 percent, larger than in any country in the world.

ational change. New generations are coming to the fore which do not necessarily share the views, values, and moods of their predecessors and may act in deliberate opposition to them. Thus, Soviet pessimism may be cyclical in character. From the regime's point of view pessimism is, of course, undesirable, but at least it reduces the danger of future disappointments caused by excessive expectations. Hopes, at present, are low: All public opinion polls and most publications show that few people expect a radical improvement in the state of the nation in the near future. As a result, the pressure on Gorbachev to perform miracles within a short time may be less than is commonly believed.

The patience shown by Russian peasants and workers throughout history is proverbial; it has been adduced time and time again as one of the most prominent ingredients of Russian national character. Russian history offers countless examples of an extraordinary readiness to suffer, to accept adverse living conditions and to obey the authorities from the days of the Tatars to the age of Stalinism. If national character were unchanging the present Soviet leadership would have little to fear. Having suffered for so long it could be expected that the Russian people might show patience for some decades.

But this can no longer be taken for granted. National character is subject to change, in the Soviet Union as elsewhere. The majority of the Soviet population consists no longer of illiterate or semiliterate workers and peasants, and the patience of the majority of the population is probably considerably shorter now than it was in the past. Under Stalin, and to a large extent also under his successors, grumbling and discontent did not greatly matter. Complaints could be expressed only in the smallest circle of friends (in the proverbial Moscow kitchen) or in the family. Public opinion had little political impact, but this is no longer so: Manifestly unpopular policies cannot be pursued in the long run without the rulers incurring considerable political risk. While expectations are now much lower among the Soviet population than they were forty years ago, so is the readiness to accept deprivation.

What happens when a religion or an ideology loses its attraction, its sway over the masses? This phenomenon has occurred frequently in the past. It has not greatly preoccupied the student of Western societies, perhaps because in these countries the existence of a religion, or a secular religion, has not been a vital necessity for the functioning of a modern society. But the Soviet Union is heir to a different tradition, and the issue is bound to be of enduring importance. The official ideology has provided legitimacy to the rulers of the Soviet Union and faith to the ruled. What can replace it, if belief has waned?

The problem has not appeared suddenly in recent years, it goes back for decades, although under *glasnost* it has become far more acute than it was before. It is not even certain whether the belief in Marxism-Leninism ever was shared by a majority of Soviet citizens, but it certainly provided a rationale and a set of beliefs for the elite. For the masses, belief in an omnipotent father figure—the dead Lenin and the living Stalin—as well as patriotism and the feeling of belonging to a community of fellow sufferers, provided the necessary cohesion. The invocation of a foreign threat, real or imaginary, always has been a most effective tool in the arsenal of Soviet propaganda. It will be recalled that at a time of supreme danger—the German attack in 1941—Stalin did not appeal to his "comrades" and the spirit of Marxism-Leninism, but instead he addressed his "brothers and sisters" and invoked patriotism.

The belief in communism was intense among young militants in the 1920s, and it continued to be effective, by and large, despite the mistakes of the leadership (such as the collectivization of agriculture and the purges) up to the outbreak of the war. Since then there has been a steady erosion; while the older militants thought back with nostalgia to the wonderful days of their youth, to an age of idealism, exalted hope, and widespread enthusiasm, these qualities were less and less evident among the young. True, they were indoctrinated in school and in the Komsomol, and they repeated their obligatory formulas after their teachers and leaders. They probably even believed in them, but the indoctrination was not deep and lasting. As soon as their critical faculties awakened, at the very latest when they left school and confronted life, they realized that there was an enormous discrepancy between theory and reality in Soviet life.

Certain ingredients of the official ideology by now are rooted deeply in Soviet mentality, but the doctrine as such has ceased to be a dynamic force. There may well be more interest in Marxism in Western universities than there is in Russia. Yet even if an ideology has lost its momentum it cannot simply be discarded; it continues to provide legitimacy to the ruling elite, to the social and political system, and to the institutions created under it. But when the official ideology no longer can act as a compass or a guide to action in domestic and foreign policy, the ruling stratum has to act pragmatically, trying to find *post-factum* justification in the writings of Lenin for the action they have taken.

This practice has been known for a long time as the "creative application" of Marxism-Leninism. It has been pursued consistently for a long time, and, as a result, the distance between the actual state of affairs of the country and the official doctrine has been widening. Words have lost their meaning or even have assumed a meaning opposite to the one originally intended. Hence, the question is asked more and more frequently: Why bother to find a justification for present-day decisions in books from a different historical period, one in which many current problems could not possibly have been anticipated?

Legitimacy is an important consideration, but true motivation is even more important. If Marxism-Leninism has lost its attraction, what other belief can replace it? Religion kept some of its hold among the older people and in the countryside even during the most severe antireligious campaigns. It had a limited revival during World War II, and there has been a reawakening of interest in religion among sections of the intelligentsia during the last two decades. The restoration of old churches has become as fashionable as the collection of icons. However, the official Russian Orthodox church is held in contempt by most intellectuals because of its close collaboration with the regime. The eagerness of many church dignitaries, especially those highly placed, to please the authorities, along with their reluctance to take risks and to endanger their positions, has greatly diminished their moral prestige.

This is much less true of the various sectarian groups, most of which were never recognized (and penetrated) to the same extent as the Orthodox church. In some parts of the Soviet Union, notably in the Baltic republics, the church has been among the leaders of the nationalistic movement; it has been the keeper of the flame, and its prestige has remained consistently high. In Central Asia, official Islam was either destroyed or coopted by the regime; thus, the door has been opened to Sufi sects about which little is known and which may play an increasingly important role in days to come.

Nevertheless, it is unlikely that outside Central Asia religion will be a decisive political factor. While it is frequently argued that the Russian people throughout history have been deeply attached to their religion, a good case can also be made for a traditional lack of religiosity, or even enmity toward it. The real motivation of the most vociferous present-day proponents of a return to religion is patriotic-nationalist rather than religious. The church is cherished because it is part of the Russian tradition. The most radical nationalists advocate a revival of pagan pre-Christian cults, as the most extreme Nazis did, but these small groups are unlikely to grow in influence.

The existence of a spiritual void is a fact of life acknowledged by virtually all knowledgeable observers of the Soviet scene, but the ability of the Orthodox church to fill this void in the coming years is doubtful. The Orthodox church is not an integrating factor, because its influence is restricted to only part of the Great Russian section of the population. Its rituals are impressive, but it has few dignitaries capable of attracting the educated sections of society. It has no distinct political and social orientation, and after its sad experiences in the past it is unlikely to try to regain its role in politics.

Religion is in demand for baptism, burial, and other such

occasions, but not as a secular mentor. The Orthodox church in its present form is not a threat to the Communist party nor to the Soviet state. On the contrary, it can be, and perhaps will be, a useful assistant in certain circumstances. All that has been said here refers to established religion in the Soviet Union; it is possible that a religious revival might still occur, with new messages preached outside established frameworks, in forms that cannot be envisaged. But indications are that there will be no turning back to a religious phase in the Soviet Union. The spiritual vacuum is not a specifically Russian phenomenon. It may be difficult to live with for many Russians, but no alternative is in sight.

NATIONALISM

The internationalist inspiration of early Bolshevism has been watered down since an early date. The writer Vasili Grossman in his famous novel, *Life and Fate,* published in the West in the 1970s and in the Soviet Union in 1988, regarded the Second World War as the great watershed between internationalism and nationalism. Already in the 1930s there were many indications of a patriotic-nationalist upsurge, which became inevitable once Stalin's policy of building socialism in one country had been adopted.

How much further will the nationalist mood spread in the years to come, and to what extent can it replace Leninism? Of all the rival ideologies, Russian nationalism is the most powerful and the most vocal. It has deep roots in the people and strong support in the bureaucracy, particularly in the army command. The Russia-firsters even now exercise powerful influence through literary magazines and patriotic clubs. Every Soviet armed forces recruit is subjected to patriotic indoctrination. There is a deep feeling that at a time of crisis only people of Russian origin can be trusted. This is based on the assumption that fatherland, native language, and common ancestry are more important than social origin, proletarian internationalism, and a dialectical materialist philosophy in which there is little room for the Russian "eternal values."

On the fringes of the Russian nationalists one encounters paranoid groups claiming that Russian culture and traditions systematically are being undermined and destroyed and that Russians ("like American Indians") are being turned into strangers in their own country. This extreme "Russian ideology" is probably no more than a nuisance, unlikely even in optimal conditions to affect more than, say, 10 to 15 percent of the population, as did the Black Hundred in Czarist Russia.

In its more moderate and respectable form, nationalism builds on a strong tradition of populism and contains an admixture of not necessarily violent xenophobia. It is widespread at present, and it could become even stronger in the future, but its spread is fraught with many dangers. Far from integrating the peoples of the Soviet Union, it is bound to divide them. Russian nationalism cannot appeal to the non-Russian half of the population as a state doctrine. It makes political sense only on the assumption that the national minorities will secede or that they will be totally assimilated. This would mean either a Russia much reduced in territory and population or a policy of forced assimilation unprecedented in history and bound to fail in the end. Neither is a practical possibility, and neither is wanted, even by the Russian patriots. This limits Russian national socialism as a factor capable of providing cohesion in a multinational empire.

True, the Soviet authorities no doubt will try to establish a common front with the Ukrainians and White Russians, in which case the united Slavic element would constitute a preponderant factor in the Soviet empire. This is not likely, however, to dampen the nationalist enthusiasm of the non-Slavic peoples and their pressure for greater sovereignty. Seen in wider perspective, the promotion of Russian nationalism or Slavic solidarity would create more difficulties than solutions, but it still may be tried. It would be an instinctive reaction in an emergency that has to be confronted by the leadership. In such situations there is no time to ponder the long-term consequences of action. Thus the importance of Russian nationalism is likely to rise despite the dangers involved.

Both neo-Marxism and liberalism have proponents in the Soviet Union, but they are not many, and their prospects are dim. There are some who believe that Marxism was never given a fair chance in Russia; the country was backward and therefore ill-suited at the time for the application of a doctrine originally meant to prevail in the most developed industrial countries. Later on, Stalinism "distorted" promising beginnings on the road to a more just society and gave socialism a bad name. However, the Soviet Union is no longer an underdeveloped country; thus, conditions are ripe for a second attempt to carry out the prescriptions of Marx and Lenin. This, broadly speaking, is the view of both the more enlightened elements among the party leadership and the tiny new leftist groups among the dissenters. But there is no popular support for designs of this kind. "Really existing social-ism" has been with the Soviet peoples for a long time, and the desire for change is much stronger than the belief that it can be modified and improved.

Desire for change will not result in the adoption of Western liberal ideas and values. Liberalism was never deeply rooted in Russian history; its influence was limited, by and large, to sections of the intelligentsia, and even among them it was adopted by only a minority. Today, the general belief is that Western style liberalism may be well-suited for certain Western societies, especially for smaller countries in which social and national conflicts are not rampant. But in a society, such as the Soviet Union, which lacks homogeneity such institutional change would be an invitation to disaster. The country has not yet reached the degree of maturity needed, nor is it likely to do so in the foreseeable future. Some leading intellectuals are preaching the virtues of greater tolerance, more freedom of speech, and common sense rather than doctrinaire fanaticism in politics, and they look with envy to the higher political culture of some European countries. Even the greatest optimists among them feel the need for a strong hand to control reforms for a long time to come. They point to the fact that virtually every change in Russian history, from the importation of potatoes onward, has been introduced by order from above, usually against much resistance.

Assuming that democratization will continue, an assumption which cannot be taken for granted, the new Soviet ideology will consist of a mixture of elements not easily compatible. Marxism-Leninism will remain the official state doctrine for want of another that could replace it, but it will provide even less true motivation than it has in the past. Like official doctrines elsewhere, it will supply texts that can be constructed in various ways, even in diametrically opposed political approaches. Ultimately, Leninism may give way to a specifically Russian brand of nationalism or populism or democracy, but this still may be a long way off.

Democratic-liberal-humanist values will be invoked by the intelligentsia more often than they have been in the past. But the intelligentsia will have to be satisfied with a greater measure of cultural rather than general political freedom. This is an unsatisfactory state of affairs, but one that is likely to be accepted by many for want of an alternative.

This seems to be the most likely prospect at the present time, but it rests on the assumption that the Soviet Union will not be shaken by major convulsions threatening the functioning of the regime in the years to come; it is by no means the only possible scenario. The case of the Soviet Union is unique in the annals of world history: A "frozen revolution," which for decades could move neither forward nor backward toward a Soviet Thermidor, has now entered a new phase of ferment. This second thaw has affected some parts of the Soviet body politic but not others. It is proceeding slowly in some crucial aspects, and the fear that it may result in an uncontrollable torrent induces the authorities to proceed with great caution. Whether they will be able to control developments is another question altogether, one which leads, by necessity, to an assessment of the centrifugal elements facing the Soviet leadership in this new, unprecedented and unforeseeable situation.

National Ferment

For almost seventy years even the critics of the Soviet system have shared the official view that, by and large, Soviet national policy has been a success, that alone among the great powers the Soviet Union has not had to undergo decolonization, and that the various nationalities have been integrated and have found their places and roles in this multinational state. True, from the early 1980s there have been signs that all was not well on the domestic front, but only since 1987 has the depth of the crisis become manifest.

The earlier optimism was not entirely unjustified; there were few outward signs of unrest or of resurgence of the nationalist movement. The organs of state security saw to that. It also was widely assumed that the central authorities had largely succeeded in winning over the native elites or in coopting at least a considerable part of them. Thus, they could safely leave the business of running the non-Russian republics to them. It apparently was not realized that, the moment police controls were reduced, nationalist forces hitherto suppressed would resurface again. Nor was it understood that the local elites, in particular in the Muslim republics, had been won over more by the promise of sharing power and material spoils than by sincere ideological conviction. They established a system of rule that had far more in common with the mafia than with the writings of Lenin, or indeed with any kind of communism, however broadly interpreted. At the same time, nationalist feelings found new, powerful expression in the non-Russian republics in the European parts of the Soviet Union. Corruption played a much smaller role in these regions, and Moscow still could count on the loyalty of at least part of the political class in White Russia and the Ukraine. But the general feeling in 1988–89 was that, to put it cautiously, the nationalities policy was in need of a drastic overhaul, that it would preoccupy increasingly the central authorities in the years to come, and that no one knew in what direction change should take place.

There had been a reluctance to confront nationalist issues in the past and consequently a lack of clarity in the minds of policy-makers, hence the recent suggestions that the best way to placate the nationalists was to raise the standard of living of the population and, perhaps, to allow more linguistic autonomy. This assumed that the wealthier Uzbeks, Armenians, and Estonians would be more content, less militant, and less likely to cause nationalist mischief. It ignored past experience in the Soviet Union and elsewhere. The Basque region in Spain and the Croatian republic in Yugoslavia are among the regions with the highest standards of living in their respective countries, but this has not had the slightest impact on the intensity of their nationalist feeling. Oppressed nationalities are sometimes also socially disadvantaged, but often they are not. Nor does the fact that most Catholic Irishmen or Basques master English or Spanish much better than they do their native language make them more friendly to the central government.

Yet even if the Soviet assumption were correct, if living conditions were the key to solving the crisis, how could it be accomplished in the foreseeable future? It is, after all, the aim of the authorities to raise the standard of living of the whole population, not just that of the militant minorities. It is clear that this will take a long time to accomplish.

Furthermore, it is obvious that the struggle for the division of national resources and income will continue and perhaps even sharpen in the future. The Baltic republics argue that they help to cover the Russian deficit but get little, if anything, in return; the Central Asians complain about discrimination. Central Asian intensive agriculture depends largely on irrigation. But as the central authorities have given in to the demands of the Siberians not to divert their rivers for this purpose, the Central Asians fear that they have been condemned to gradual impoverishment; the region with the greatest population growth in the Soviet Union will not have enough water to develop its agriculture.

However, the basic problems underlying national dissent are not economic, but rather political and cultural. The idea that the local elites had been won over proved to be an illusion. That a

Russian rather than a Kazakh had to be appointed first secretary of the party in Alma Ata, and that for the first time in many years no Central Asian was found in the Politburo, were admissions of failure. There are various ways to confront the national issues— concession, repression, or a mixture of the two—but a return *tout court* to Stalinist methods is ruled out. Any repression less drastic is unlikely to succeed.

Had the Soviet leadership granted the major nationalities far reaching concessions regarding power-sharing in the 1980s, if genuine decentralization would have taken place as, for instance, in pre-1914 Austria-Hungary, such an approach might have worked in most, if not perhaps in all, cases. The republics in the European part of the Soviet Union, except only the RSFSR and the Ukraine, are probably too small to be viable. There are many Russians living in these non-Russian republics and even if most of them would leave, the economies of these republics would still depend on the Russian market and the supply of raw materials from the RSFSR. The dependence of the Central Asian republics on the RSFSR is equally obvious. (A united Baltic republic might be in a stronger position; it would be more populous than Finland but its survival would still be precarious for a variety of reasons.)

However, the opportunity to give the republics a greater measure of real sovereignty was missed by the Politburo and the question arises whether such a chance will still exist in the 1990s. The movement for full, or nearly complete, independence has immeasurably grown in many republics, quite irrespective of the uncertainties and dangers involved. At the same time both among the Russian liberals and the conservatives there is greater willingness to accede to the demands of the secessionists at least in some of the republics. But this will be done only at a price. This refers to military bases, guarantees concerning the status of the Russian minorities in the republics, as well as economic demands.

The negotiations concerning independence will be protracted and the Soviet leadership assumes, not perhaps without reason, that more moderate views will prevail among the nationalities concerning the dangers of Balkanization. In other words, it is hoped that they may be willing to accept eventually something short of full independence.

What future is there for a sovereign Armenia or Georgia? Although the Soviet Union does not accept the Armenian claims to Nagorno-Karabakh, it is nevertheless Armenia's traditional protector against neighboring Turkey, their sworn foe (and militantly Islamic Iran is no more sympathetic). Armenian, unlike Baltic, nationalism collides not so much with Russia as with neighboring Azerbaidjan. Georgia's complaints are mainly cultural-political (Russification), and there is also the longstanding demand for noninterference. The same is true with regard to the Ukraine, with the exception of western Ukraine where separatist aspirations, intensified by religious dissent have been traditionally strong. However, Ukrainian nationalism has been opposed historically to Poland at least as much as to Russia, and its cultural demands are not unfulfillable from a Russian point of view.

If the Soviet Union faced only its European and Caucasian minorities the problems would still be manageable. True, the alienation of the Armenians might have unpleasant consequences; in the Armenian diaspora pro-Soviet sympathies have been quite strong, and the Russians are likely to lose this goodwill. No country has been able to reconcile the conflicting claims of all of its components. The Soviet leadership is no exception, but such antagonisms have not caused the breakdown of all multinational states.

Within the next years a potentially dangerous situation will develop in Central Asia. At the present time it is more a matter of sporadic outbreaks and passive resistance rather than an Islamic or nationalist revival. However, it is unclear to what extent the present leadership is still in control of the political lives of the Central Asian nationalities. The clashes that have taken place in cities such as Fergana and Alma Ata have not spread widely; the crucial question is not whether they may recur (which, given the existing tensions, seems almost inevitable) but whether they will turn into violent conflict on a mass scale as has occurred in other parts of the world.

The impact of the religious revival in Central Asia has been overrated. Khomeinism will not find fertile ground there, partly because most of these republics are Sunni rather than Shiite. The setback of Khomeinism in Iran, and the fact that the standard of living and general cultural level in Soviet Central Asia are higher than in Afghanistan and Iran, are further barriers. But Muslim sectarianism combined with the desire to maintain the traditional way of life still may create grave political problems in the years to come. Either the Soviet authorities can revert to the old Leonid Brezhnev strategy of ignoring the tensions and preserving a semblance of order by letting local chieftains run the republics as they see fit, or they can try to introduce and maintain Soviet norms of political and cultural behavior. This is bound, however, to lead to new confrontations.

Ferment in Central Asia in the years to come is far more likely to be nationalist rather than religious in motivation. To be precise, it will be predominantly nationalist with a strong traditional religious admixture. A common front of the Central Asian nationalities is unlikely to become an effective political factor, and this reduces the threat as far as Moscow is concerned. While the nationalities share some common traditions and aspirations, their interests by no means always coincide. In a Central Asian union, the Uzbeks would predominate, and this would not be welcomed by the others. The Kazakhs and Kirgiz have often quarrelled, and the relations between the other nationalities also have not been free of friction. The Russian presence in Central Asia has shrunk over the last decade, partly as a result of unsatisfactory ethnic relations, but it is still considerable. Together with Ukrainian settlers, their number in Kazakhstan is about as great as that of the Kazakhs. It seems likely that in most major cities of Central Asia there are more Russians than there are members of any other nationality.

In this important respect the situation differs from that which has faced other imperial nations. The closest parallel would be perhaps with Algeria in the 1950s, except that the number of Russians is much larger, the "colony" is not separated from the metropolis by hundreds of miles, and the "natives" cannot count on effective help from their coreligionists beyond the border.

Secession and the emergence of one or more independent Central Asian republics is therefore unlikely in the near future, but continued Soviet rule will perpetuate and probably aggravate existing tensions. Home rule would be a possible option only if there were a substantial number of reliable native Communists, but such a political class seems not to exist. In its absence, home rule would mean a system of government with more in common with Third World Middle Eastern practices and customs than with the Soviet model. It would lead, in all probability, to the exodus of most Russians and members of other nonnative nationalities from Central Asia. Such regimes, even if they were to pay lip service to the Moscow leadership, could not be considered reliable.

The alternatives are equally unsatisfactory: Direct rule from Moscow, even if it results in material benefits such as better housing conditions and supplies, will not bring greater friendship between the peoples. Furthermore, the question of how to handle the growing number of Central Asian recruits in the Soviet army will continue. This specific problem perhaps could be alleviated by letting Central Asian recruits serve in their native republics or even by letting them serve for shorter periods. Such discrimination would, however, almost certainly trigger demands for similar treatment in other parts of the Soviet Union.

There is no solution for the Central Asian problems in the foreseeable future. If they are handled by Moscow with a wrong, tactless, politically shortsighted policy, the situation could aggravate within a short time. Even a clever, farsighted, sophisticated strategy might not be successful except to the extent of its preventing an acute outbreak of nationalist passions. The central Soviet government probably will pursue a firm line yet try not to provoke the nationalities. Given the demographic trends and the unwillingness of the nationalities to become Russified or to share power with their non-Muslim neighbors, the most the central authorities can hope for is a decade or two of uneasy coexistence.

A sullen native population will show little enthusiasm for pulling its weight as far as the reform policy, or indeed any policy emanating from Moscow, is concerned. The Soviet leadership has at present no clear concept of how to conduct its policy in Central Asia, and no such grand design is in sight. In the meantime policy will be shaped by pragmatic considerations of trying to maintain Soviet rule with a minimum of risk and friction.

Social Ferment

According to official Soviet spokesmen the economic situation is unlikely to improve substantially within the next two or three years, that is to say before the beginning of a new five-year plan. The utility of such plans is doubted by Soviet economists, and it is quite likely that planning strategies will be substantially changed. According to more realistic appraisals, genuine improvement may take ten years or even longer. Will the Soviet population give political credit to their government for so long a period? The regime has little to fear from the peasants; their situation, particularly in the nonblack-soil zone of Russia, has been deplorable. Whether the farm reforms will work is uncertain, but, even if they should not, an agricultural laborers' revolt is quite unlikely. Discontent in the countryside has manifested itself in a growing exodus of farmers leaving for the big cities, not in protest demonstrations and other political forms of action. This is unlikely to change in the near future, since peasants usually find it difficult to get organized and to take collective action.

The state of the working class seems to be quite different in this respect, although admittedly less is known about workers in the Soviet Union than is known about any other class. While conditions in the countryside have been studied carefully, and even small and exotic nationalities have been investigated thoroughly, very little is known about working class life, the mood of the workers, and their hopes, fears, and aspirations. Neither sociologists nor novelists, journalists nor party officials seem to be well informed about the subject. In fact, it is not at all certain to what extent the working class has escaped party control. The income of workers improved under Leonid Brezhnev relative to other sections of the population, but there is no reason to assume that complaints have become fewer. Unsatisfactory working and housing conditions, shortages in essential supplies, waiting in lines for many hours each week, the deterioration of social services—there has been no essential change in these conditions under Gorbachev. On the contrary, there are new complaints concerning the unavailability or the high cost of essential commodities and services as well as resentment of the new cooperatives, which are believed to enrich themselves by exploiting other sections of the population. Workers fear price rises and possible unemployment as the result of economic reform.

Economic reform is unpopular among the workers who assume, not without reason, that for years to come it will mean higher productivity (that is to say, greater effort) for the same renumeration as before, or perhaps for even lower real wages. The command economy may not be popular among the intellectuals, but it still has supporters among the workers, who have become accustomed to job security and state subsidies for food staples. Any attempt to tamper with these subsidies is bound to stir up unrest. There is much discontent among younger workers confronted with boredom and the lack of entertainment in most Soviet cities. They may earn relatively good wages, but there is no way to spend the money.

The authorities have learned from local strikes as well as from the experience of other Communist countries, such as the political storm created by the Polish government's attempts at price reform. Nevertheless, the subsidies will have to be cut in the long run, and the regime then will enter a period of high political risk. The risk can be somewhat reduced by importing consumer goods from abroad, thus creating greater incentives. The most militant and strategically important sections of the working class perhaps can be appeased with higher bonuses or preferential supplies, but those who are comparatively defenseless will have to bear the brunt of the reforms. The considerable regional differences in working class income and supply of goods also should be taken into account. It also might be possible to deflect discontent from its real causes and direct it against imaginary targets: the "enemy" that threatens the Soviet Union and forces it to spend so much on national defense, or mythical internal enemies. This would be a counsel of despair for which a high price would have to be paid. It would be tantamount to the liquidation of the reform policy, a return to the state of affairs before 1986.

If essential goods remain in short supply or have to be rationed, or if lines for food should grow, there will be a danger of demonstrations and riots which, given the greater openness in political life, could spread as they have done in revolutionary situations before. (The last writer to deal with this phenomenon was Alexander Solzhenitsyn in *The Red Wheel*, his book on March 1917.) Workers can organize themselves much more easily than can other social classes, so the idea of independent trade unions or independent soviets might fall on fertile ground. At the same time slogans such as "We had it better under Stalin" (or even Brezhnev) might spread.

Few workers of today remember what conditions were like under Stalin, and even the dream of the good old days of Brezhnev takes one back almost a quarter of a century. It is the perception that counts, and Soviet working class perceptions are essentially conservative: fear of change and resentment against those who earn more because of initiative, effort, or inventiveness. A protest movement could compel the regime to retreat from its reform policy. It has caused certain personnel changes in the regional and national leadership. Could it bring down the regime? Attempts have been made by the opponents of reform to mobilize the workers against *perestroika*. Such initiatives will, no doubt, continue in future. Various local and even nationwide organizations have been founded, demanding more power to the workers, putting the blame for their low living standards and acute shortages on the liberal intelligentsia. The forces behind these initiatives appeal to the strong egalitarian bias among the masses and the detestation of private initiative, market forces, et cetera. However, the workers are not sufficiently naive to believe that the old economic system would work better, nor do they accept that patriotic slogans will improve the supply situation. Nevertheless, such populist appeals should not be underrated, since sentiments of this kind are probably shared by a majority of people. They can slow down reform or even bring it to a halt, even if they have no alternatives to offer.

If a map were drawn of the anti-reform forces that might play an important role in coming political showdowns, one would probably find geographical factors of greater significance than old-fashioned "class struggle." Polarization is most pronounced and anti-reform forces strongest in declining cities and regions with outdated industries and law and order problems (Kazan). This refers in particular to Leningrad but also to some of the major cities in the Volga region, the Ural and Siberia, and perhaps White Russia (called by some the Russian Vendée), as well as other centers in which supplies have been traditionally unsatisfactory. Local cases of unrest could be contained. But a serious situation would arise if it were to spread, and a transport workers strike would be even more dangerous if it lasted for any length of time.

The authorities may know little about the mood of the workers, but they would not remain insensitive if unrest should occur. They have much experience in political manipulation. Propaganda alone, needless to say, would have little effect in such a situation except perhaps in the short run. A shake-up of the system within its present boundaries, campaigns to stamp out corruption and inefficiency, and insistence on greater discipline are palliatives that have been tried many times, but they never have had more than short-term results. The regime might adopt policies popular with one part of the population but not the other: a currency reform, for instance, such as after World War II. This would hit those who have saved money (or earned it in the second economy), but it would not affect the poorer sections. However, such measures would demoralize the more active sections of the population. The little time it might gain for the regime would be at the expense of its long-term goals. The authorities would find themselves in a position in which old methods no longer work, but a new approach cannot be adopted because of political resistance. This would mean either abdication and more *zastoi* (stagnation) or the adoption of more stringent policies, another "revolution from above," and more dictatorship.

The Intelligentsia

The role of the intellectuals and the young generation in the current political and social ferment ought to be mentioned at least in passing. The former head of the KGB and others of the same persuasion have warned against destabilizing trends, and there is a grain of truth in these warnings. The stream of revelations about the past which has come forth undermines the belief in the kind of system the conservatives want to preserve. True, the views of the liberals are by no means shared by all members of the intelligentsia, especially outside Moscow and Leningrad, but their radicalism is a matter of great concern for the antireformers.

The first thaw was stopped easily enough, partly under Nikita Khrushchev and then altogether under Brezhnev. A reversal of *glasnost* in present circumstances, while not impossible in principle, would be far more difficult. The Polish example—and to a lesser degree that of East Germany—has shown that a Communist regime can survive for a number of years while largely ignoring the intelligentsia. Some collaborators can always be found, and the radicals can be isolated so that their impact on society will be small. Or, to put it a different way, greater cultural freedom can coexist with political repression as far as most of the people are concerned. The Czarist regime survived despite the bitter hostility of most of the intelligentsia, and the Communist regime is far better equipped to survive in similar circumstances.

But the Soviet Union is not Albania. A policy alienating the intelligentsia would have dire consequences over the years. It would reduce the Soviet regime to a system of government devoid of legitimacy and based on the self-interest of the *nomenklatura* and others who materially benefit from the regime. Such a regime would grow progressively weaker and eventually disintegrate.

There are alternative strategies. The intelligentsia might be persuaded to accept an arrangement in which its freedom is not paralleled by freedom of other sections of the population. The government could stress that the desire for *glasnost* and democratization is not shared in equal measure by other classes and that there is much anti-intellectualism among wide sections of the population. Unlike its counterpart in Poland, between 1981–89 the Soviet government might well obtain a measure of cooperation from the intelligentsia.

A more conservative leadership than the present one is not likely to make a major effort to gain the goodwill of the intellectuals, nor would such an effort, if undertaken, be very successful. But even they probably would have some intellectual support, especially from among the nationalists. A more enlightened leadership will not greatly fear the mainstream intelligentsia. It will be confident that the system is strong enough to survive all kinds of revelations about the past and that, in any case, the novelty of the revelations will wear off within a few years from now.

The young generation is more difficult to handle. Once the main hope of the Soviet regime, it has become the source of much apprehension. It has become not anti-Soviet but non-Soviet, having opted to a large extent out of the system. Official indoctrination has not worked for a long time, and the system has lost its attraction. An independent youth culture has emerged, featuring all kinds of fads and fashions, many of them Western in origin. The young generation largely is devoid of belief in the Communist cause, bored by politics, and become even more materialistic than their more affluent contemporaries in the West. True, there are idealists among them, but they are a minority and do not shape the face of a generation about which some Soviet officials have said, "We have lost them."

Will they be able to regain their confidence? It seems unlikely, short of a new and powerful spiritual message to provide motivation. In the meantime there has been little active resistance among the youth, except perhaps among the national minorities. Young people have not played a prominent role in the political struggle, unlike in Czarist Russia, when students were in the forefront of protest movements. At present the most pronounced features of Soviet youth are political indifference and preoccupation with the private sphere of life.

Is this likely to remain so forever? The alternative youth culture rejects most of the official values. The authorities nevertheless have evaded carefully a head-on collision with the young generation. Potentially, Soviet youth could be the most important single factor in the struggle for the future of the Soviet Union. But unless it can be mobilized, its role will not change soon. One of the features of youth revolt is that it occurs suddenly, without warning and for no obvious reason, except perhaps boredom or some provocation by the powers that be. Youth revolt is usually shortlived and seldom politically decisive, but in combination with other forces in society it suddenly could take its place in the vanguard of a political movement.

Forces of Cohesion

Enough has been said about the forces likely to cause ferment and disruption in the Soviet Union. The opposite camp, that of those who are vitally interested in keeping the system unchanged, seems to be stronger at least for the time being. It consists of the party's inner hard core, otherwise known as the party apparatus (not the rank-and-file party members who do not participate in decision making). It refers not so much to the *nomenklatura*, which includes not a few reformist individuals, but to the middle echelons of the bureaucracy—not just the "generals," as Stalin called them, but the party and state officer corps, the state party armed-forces state security complex. Within this complex are considerable differences of view and clashes of interest, but all of its elements share the convictions that the system must be preserved and that domestic social and national disintegration must be stopped, by draconic means if necessary. These forces are not necessarily against change, but they want gradual, slow, orderly change within parameters set by themselves. If this is not possible, they will opt for a return to the traditional style of government, putting an end to the promises of democratization.

The Polish example between 1981 and 1989 and also the Chinese example in June of 1989 have shown that such a solution is perfectly possible, even in a country in which communism is less deeply rooted than it is in Russia and where the forces opposing the regime are stronger. A price must be paid for a government of "national salvation," as in Poland; the Communist party will play a less prominent part, and since neither the state bureaucracy nor the organs of state security enjoy a great deal of prestige the army is bound, by elimination, to take a leading part in a regime of this kind. There are two obstacles to overcome: The army commanders have not been trained to provide political leadership, and they have little to offer as a new message except Russian patriotism. This will not be sufficient to steer the country through the complex social problems facing it.

Furthermore, it would mean the final abdication of Communist ideology, however liberally interpreted. There is nothing in Marx, Lenin, or even Stalin providing for a military dictatorship, as in Poland under martial law, seventy-five years after the Revolution. True, it could be argued that the army commanders are only party members in uniform and that their rule is not directed against the working class or the intelligentsia; rather they constitute an independent force in society with the temporary assignment of saving the country from disaster.

One should not underrate the potential initial popularity of such a regime, especially if it should come to power after a period of grave unrest threatening the existence of Soviet society and state—mass strikes, demonstrations, clashes with the police, and secessionist movements among the nationalities. In such a situation, a great many people would accept a government of this kind with relief, if not with enthusiasm. It also can be predicted with near certainty that such a government would achieve nothing except the restoration of public order and the outward semblance of normality. There is the remote possibility that out of such a government one exceptionally gifted leader—a late twentieth-century Napoleon Bonaparte—or perhaps a small group of leaders, would emerge and use the opportunity to carry out yet another revolution from above, changing the character of the regime. It is perfectly true that it is much easier to carry out far-reaching changes, such as dismantling institutions or pushing through ideological changes, in a state of emergency. But the odds against a Soviet Thermidor, in whatever direction, are heavy. It might be relatively easy to suppress all opposition, because all the levers of power would be in the hands of the forces of order. It would mean a return to a command economy and a command society permeated by nepotism and corruption, a revival of Brezhnevism more energetically applied.

It would be highly desirable, from the party leadership's point of view, if it could confront a serious internal crisis without giving the army and the KGB a larger say in policymaking. Special police units have been created by the Ministry of Interior, but it is doubtful whether these forces would be adequate in the case of a widespread breakdown of public order. The Soviet armed forces were used to arrest Lavrenty Pavlovich Beria and to get rid of the "anti-party group" under Khrushchev. A future contingency might be essentially different, however, inasmuch as the army might be needed not just for a specific action but for a much longer period to maintain order and to give legitimacy to the regime. This would be unsatisfactory, and not just from an ideological and prestige point of view. It has been the golden rule throughout the Soviet period to keep the armed forces under tight party control. The same has been true with regard to the security forces, at least since 1953. Once the military leaders are accepted as partners in running the country, it may be difficult to persuade them to return to their bases and barracks once the emergency has passed.

It follows that, if a critical situation arises, an attempt will be made to confront it first by traditional means, with the party in charge and the army and security organs merely executing its orders. If the situation is not very dangerous, the traditional approach could be sufficient. In a real emergency, though, the party leadership might be compelled, however reluctantly, to accept ways and means to save the system that would be fraught with danger for its own predominant role in Soviet political and social life.

Substantial change in the Soviet Union may happen, broadly speaking, in two different ways: over a long period of time, or as a result of a sudden, severe crisis threatening the very existence of the regime. At present, the former scenario still seems more likely. No system is immune to change, but change very often takes considerably longer than most analysts (and prophets) realize. It is easy to point to trends that indicate impending change, while the many retarding factors are often hidden from the eye and thus ignored or underrated.

The issue of generational change is important. The Soviet Union still is ruled today by men who joined the Communist party under Stalin or who grew up in the Stalinist tradition. Twenty years from now, those who were born around 1960 will be moving into key positions. While it is impossible to predict their ideological orientation, it seems obvious that their attitudes will be different. They will be much less weighed down by past traditions, and it will be easier for them to move in any direction. The same will be true not only of the leadership but also of the rest of the population. Options that politically and psychologically are excluded today at least will be discussed, and probably will be tried, with the emergence of a new generation. These options are not limitless; they will have to be in some accordance with Russian and Soviet heritage and existing institutions. Marxism-Leninism will be discarded gradually or transformed into a nationalist and populist ideology more in line with Soviet realities. In the meantime, the most that can be expected is a policy of little steps forward, a policy very likely to be interrupted by threats and setbacks.

The second, less likely, scenario might be a cultural revolution. This implies not only a change of heart among the leaders, the introduction of new policies, and the establishment of new institutions, but also a sea change in mentality and motivation among the people, or at least among considerable sections of the population. It implies, to put it somewhat imprecisely, a change in national character. A cultural revolution could recapture the revolutionary enthusiasm and idealism that were found among the political elite in the 1920s. Alternatively, it could generate new enthusiasm as the result of some powerful political message with quasi-religious appeal, calling the faithful to build heaven on earth. It has been noted that such cultural revolutions, not just changing the political leadership but having much deeper effects, are exceedingly rare in the history of nations. Far more often than not they fail, as happened in China. A development of this kind in the Soviet Union would be a near-miracle.

Change also could result from a major shock. This cannot be ruled out, but it implies the presence of a severe crisis, a clear and present danger, and the conviction held not just by part of the elite but by the majority of the population that there has to be a radical break with past policies and institutions. Such a situation sometimes arises in a war, in particular after a heavy defeat or a civil war. A major war involving the Soviet Union seems virtually impossible, but a severe crisis still could come about as the result of disasters such as widespread starvation, repeated economic setbacks causing defeatism or even panic among the people, or major government failures such as policies that having raised high hopes among the population, fail to deliver what they have promised. This refers, quite obviously, to much greater misfortunes than temporary difficulties with supplies of consumer goods or failure in Afghanistan.

Perhaps the presence of a creeping malaise and the absence of a truly frightening immediate threat made reform in the Soviet Union so difficult. There is still the hope that one could perhaps somehow muddle through and that painful, far-reaching changes could be evaded. In the 1990s, as a result of a sudden breakdown or, perhaps more likely, as the result of several breakdowns in various fields, a climate of real danger and feeling of urgency might arise. Then, the government in power, or the forces replacing it, might be able to push through reform policies that would be unthinkable in other circumstances.

The alternative to far-reaching change is business as usual—more stagnation, or tampering with the system without really changing it—if the resistance to change is still too great. Such a state of affairs cannot go on forever, but it has continued for five years and may go on for some more. It frequently is argued that accelerated change is imperative, because otherwise the Soviet Union will fall further behind the other industrialized nations. But such a decline would be relative (the Soviet Union will still be a superpower), and it would be slow. Similar predictions of decline have been made about the United States and other Western countries without causing a great deal of alarm in public opinion. It is true that the problems of the Soviet Union are of a different magnitude, but much will depend on the international context, on the situation of the other major powers. Overall stagnation does not preclude progress in some respects.

Of all major nations, the Soviet Union is the most conservative, as far as its basic attitudes and aversion to change are concerned. In recent Russian history, only Stalin achieved lasting changes. But Stalinism cannot be resurrected, and even if it could it would fail to cope with the problems of the 1990s. The battle for change in the Soviet Union will be, in all probability, an agonizingly slow one in accordance with the tradition and mood of the country. It has at long last become true that (to quote the "Internationale") neither God nor a supreme leader will bring salvation to the Soviet Union; it can be accomplished only through its own efforts. Like Baron Munchhausen in the famous story, they have to draw themselves by their own hair out from the morass.

The Impact of Domestic Affairs on Soviet Foreign Policy

The last question to be addressed concerns the likely impact of Soviet domestic affairs on the conduct of foreign and military affairs. According to widespread popular belief, a rich country will be content, unlikely to engage in aggressive foreign political ventures, whereas a poor one, having suffered setbacks and disappointments, will be tempted to improve its fortunes by wars of conquest. Sometimes this may be true, but history has not always validated this simplistic notion. Aggressive foreign policies and wars of conquest are not always motivated by overall design, and economic factors are seldom, if ever, the only decisive ones. Even in Hitler's case, nationalist motivations and the desire for revenge for the peace treaties imposed after World War I were at least as powerful inducements as the wish to acquire raw materials and markets for Germany.

The Soviet Union has no need for additional farmland, and it possesses more reserves of raw materials than all its neighbors taken together. Oil might be the only exception, but the need for it will not be so pressing in the near future as to justify the risks of military expansion. Escape into military adventures as the result of major failures on the home front seems most unlikely in the foreseeable future. Even under a government in which the military plays an important role, such a danger seems not at all imminent. The mood of the country in the 1990s is inward looking, skeptical to a certain extent, even pacifist. No amount of patriotic indoctrination is likely to swing the population toward an aggressive foreign policy. There is a preoccupation with the standard of living and the quality of life and a deep-seated wish to live in peace rather than to engage in global missions, be they Communist-ideological or Russian-imperialist. The fantasies of the militants of the late 1920s about "watering our horses in the

Ganges" have become a butt of ridicule and cannot be resuscitated.

The loss of the East European empire in 1989 was not a tremendous shock for the great majority of Soviet citizens. It may still be used one day against the Gorbachev leadership, but for a great variety of reasons the impact was not remotely as painful as the loss of empire for Britain and France, or even Belgium and Holland.

The Soviet Union still could be drawn into foreign political adventures, such as local conflicts that might spread, once the lessons of Afghanistan are forgotten. A power vacuum might come into being somewhere not far from the borders of the Soviet Union, say in the Middle East. The leadership then may stumble into a conflict, either because it feels threatened or because it thinks that it might be possible to expand the Soviet sphere of influence without risk, not out of calculation or deep desire but because of a breakdown in the international order. Such a danger, however remote, can never entirely be ruled out, but there is no connection between this and the Soviet internal state of affairs. Such a situation could arise under a conservative as well as a reformist leadership, and it could happen in conditions of domestic success as well as failure.

Soviet Visions of the Future

Since the rise of Gorbachev and the proclamation of *perestroika*, many voices have been heard inside the Soviet Union advocating a variety of policies to be adopted, warning against other courses of action, and predicting what was likely to happen in either case. The very fact that such advice has been given, such hopes and fears expressed, is, of course, a great novelty: Prior to this, there had been no policy discussions since the 1920s.

While the main participants in the early discussions covering the more technical aspects of public policy such as economic and financial problems—were professionals (that is to say, economists), it was on the whole a truly popular debate. The main spokesmen representing the right on economic matters were a theatrical producer and a railway specialist. Among prominent participants on the left were experts on the U.S. economy and on the history of the renaissance, several philosophers, and journalists. No politicians and only a few political thinkers participated in the debate. Politicians no doubt felt constrained by party discipline from voicing opinions radically different from the official party line. Political thinkers hardly had existed in the Soviet Union for a long time; those who wrote on politics had been expected to interpret the party line, not to suggest alternative policies. Political futurology had been altogether discouraged.

Under these circumstances, it was by no means surprising that fresh ideas, policy analysis, and predictions came mainly from outside the profession and from individuals whose names were not at all familiar or whose reputations were in different fields. Nor was it surprising that some contributions to the debate were not well informed or logically consistent and had little to do with the political, social, and economic problems facing the country.

It was much more remarkable that, in a country with no tradition of open political discussion, there appeared, quite suddenly, an impressive amount of knowledge, political sophistication, and even new thinking. Certain names became household words on the basis of just one article. Although these articles that made their authors famous were usually long, probably too long, this was a hallowed tradition in Russia. Since the attention span of Soviet readers is definitely greater than that of Western readers, no harm was done.

Many contributions to the national debates dealt with recent history: What had gone wrong, and why? These are of less interest in the present context than the assessments made and the policies proposed concerning the future. True, the policy prescriptions usually were based on an analysis of past mistakes and present conditions, but some contributions to the national debate focused more heavily on the past than on the future. It is with the latter that we shall be concerned here.

In the beginning of *perestroika*, its leading spokesmen from Gorbachev downward predicted that the changes would give their first fruits within three or four years, that the situation was "pre-crisis" rather than critical. This mood yielded to skepticism and even grim despair as those first years passed and the economy further deteriorated. *Perestroika* was in the beginning little more than a vague concept based on several basic assumptions: that there had been too much bureaucratic interference from the center, that greater leeway should be given to local initiative, that something akin to a second NEP was needed, with new incentives to agriculturists as well as cooperatives in town.

By 1989 it was admitted freely that mistakes had been made during the early stage of *perestroika*—for instance, with regard to the ban on vodka. The changes proved far more difficult than anticipated. There was popular resistance against higher prices and growing social inequality, the inevitable concomitant of eco-nomic liberalization. The low prices on the world market for gasoline and natural gas deprived the country of a sizable part of its expected foreign currency income. The Chernobyl disaster and the Armenian earthquake were further burdens on the economy, while strife between the nationalities and other negative social trends such as the growing crime rate contributed to growing pessimism and fears that the whole social fabric would come apart. Alexander Kabakov's *Nevozvrazhenets,* written early in the summer of 1988, was one of the first antiutopias describing (in the form of a film scenario) what life in the Soviet Union might be like in the 1990s if the general disintegration continued and the anti-*perestroika* forces had their way.[2]

Still, countervailing forces also affected the general mood. The opening of the first partly freely elected Soviet parliament in

---

[2]*Iskustvo Kino* 6, 1989, pp. 150–76.

summer 1989 and its subsequent sessions provided nationwide training in political democracy. The sessions, followed with rapt attention all over the country, provided a safety valve, but as the speeches and resolutions did not bring quick and radical change, the impact of these lessons in democracy decreased. The mood in the winter of discontent of 1989–90 was certainly far more somber than the expectations three years earlier, when almost anything had seemed possible. The conviction grew in all parts of the political spectrum that in most important respects there would be no radical improvement for years, perhaps many years, to come. Hence, the corollary: How much credit had the present party leadership? How long would the people put up with the prevailing situation—or a possible deterioration? Would the present leadership stay in power? If not, was it impossible to avoid a backlash, a reimposition of the old system? Could national strife be contained, and, if so, at what price? These were some of the main issues discussed, with widely differing assessments and expectations, inside the party as well as outside its ranks.

The Fears of the Right

The right wing, the critics and enemies of reforms, were deeply divided on essential beliefs, but they still agreed on a variety of assumptions. The country had been brought to the brink of abyss. Unless the mechanism of "sliding down"[3] was reversed, all would end in total disaster. There was no unanimity as to what form the catastrophe would take: Strikes, civil war, separatism, starvation, indiscriminate terror, and other calamities all were mentioned. (Significantly, attack by a foreign enemy was seldom mentioned.) All agreed that unless some (unspecified) decisive action was taken soon, the country faced total ruin. There was also agreement that criticism of the army and the security forces had to

---

[3]This was the title of a series of essays by Sergei Kurginian published in *Literaturnaia Rossia* between June 30 and September 1, 1989.

stop, because the army was the only force that could prevent bloodshed and preserve the territorial integrity of the Soviet Union.

The spokesmen of the right further agreed that the socioeconomic future facing the country was grim and that it was dangerous to make promises that could not be fulfilled. The ideal was not a turn to the market and consumerism, but a return to a society whose aspirations were based on spiritual values and ideals and, by necessity, an ascetic life-style. The desire to ape Western economies and life-styles could lead only to further decline, not to a West European or Japanese, but rather a Latin American standard of living.

The right was also nearly unanimous in asserting that the present critical situation and the mistaken plans for the future were largely the fault of the pro-Western intelligentsia. These allegations were not obvious, for neither under Khrushchev, nor under Brezhnev, nor even under Gorbachev, had intellectuals played any significant political role. They had made policy suggestions, but the final decisions had always been made by the political leadership.

The right-wing ideologists devoted much more time and thought to warnings against policies that should *not* be pursued than to constructive proposals. One of their number, Mikhail Antonov, emerged in 1987–1989 as one of the most prominent and prolific spokesmen of the right on socioeconomic affairs. His ideas for the future of the country are stated in an eighty-page essay, *Vykhod yest!* (There is a way out!), published in 1989 (*Nash Sovremennik* 8 and 9, 1989). His main constructive idea was a simple proposition: People have to be taught that materialism is bad, and for this they need a spiritual-patriotic-religious renaissance. The following excerpt gives a fairly clear idea of the apocalyptic outlook shared by Antonov and his sympathizers:

> If (our) Westerners prevail during the first stage, this will be a mere Pyrrhic victory. Soon they will come to regret it and their own children will curse them. The 'Westerners' have lost the

struggle from the very beginning. They believe that the main things in life are material blessings, power and money, whereas humanism is the real wealth, faith, charity and love; more and more people will come to understand this. The approach of the 'Westerners' leads into a dead end, to a general disaster. Their assumption that the West will continue to exist, polluting our country will not materialize. The world is one and the destruction of Russia, this 'ecumenical martyr,' will be merely the prelude to a cosmic disaster.

The mixture of traditional extreme right-wing doctrine and Green ideology is by no means uniquely Russian, but nowhere else has it been stated so emphatically and in so primitive a way.

The right-wingers did not agree among themselves about policies to be adopted. One school of thought, mainly neo-Stalinist in inspiration, suggested that the centralized, command economy should be maintained, the armed forces should be kept strong, the rebelling minorities suppressed without mercy, and the working class mobilized against the liberal intellectuals. But another conservative school of thought, less inspired by the Leninist-Stalinist heritage, suggested a Stolypinist orientation: Remove the fetters that were the undoing of agriculture, make the peasant the owner of his land, give more scope to initiative in the urban economy, and prevent enrichment of parasitic and criminal elements.[4] One author noted that some 20 percent of the new cooperatives were run by mafiosi, an estimate that may not have been far from the truth.

But Russia in Stolypin's time had been a predominantly agrarian country, and this was no longer true. A reorientation toward agriculture was not a practical economic proposition. While neo-Stalinists, such as the Leningrad teacher Nina Andreyeva, who had attained great notoriety in 1988, attacked Gorbachev and other reformists for allegedly betraying socialism ("as Dubcek had

---

[4]Pyotr Stolypin (1862–1911), prime minister and minister of the interior, was the ablest politician of the late Czarist era.

done in Czechoslovakia"), the non-Communist conservatives, on the contrary, condemned not just Marxism-Leninism but social-ism *tout court* as contrary to human nature, Russian values and traditions, and the whole spirit of the nation. Some, like the mathematician Igor Shafarevich, did so openly, others did so by implication, by constant invocation of prerevolutionary (and an-tirevolutionary) authors and writings. One could still find a com-mon anticapitalist, populist, solidarist denominator among these various schools of thought on the right, but for outlining policy options for the years ahead there could be no common language.

Mention has been made of the strong anti-Western, antilib-eral, anti-Jewish, and masonic elements in the mental composi-tion of the Russian right. Ideological anti-Westernism is mostly limited to small groups of right-wing intellectuals, and there is no alternative orientation toward the East in the tradition of the Eurasian philosophers of the 1920s. (Their East was, in any case, an abstract concept, not a political reality.)

It is true that some Russians believe that "Western ways are not for us" and that, in any case, the negative aspects of Western civilization should not be allowed to contaminate the Russian people. But the phenomenal success of Western mass culture in the Soviet Union shows that the fascination with the West is much stronger than any other alternative orientation, and it is likely to remain so. More intensive patriotic indoctrination will not change this. Some Russian nationalists may admire the Khomeinism and Muslim fundamentalism for their intense belief and consistency in contrast to the decadent West, but they still have no wish to convert to Islam.

The demographic trends provide reason for fear. According to preliminary results of the 1989 census the population of the Central Asian republics is now 11.5 percent of the population of the Soviet Union, in comparison with 6.6 percent in 1959. Inside Central Asia the percentage of the native population has grown even more quickly, and this is, of course, of great political signifi-cance. Whereas the rate of childbirth among young Russian, Ukrainian, and Byelorussian women who were married in the early 1980s is projected at less than two children per woman, Central Asian women of the same age bracket are expected to have an average of five children. The Slavic element of the Soviet Union is declining both relatively and absolutely.

Complaints about economic discrimination against ethnic Russians are correct in that the Central Asian republics are subsidized at the rate of 6 billion rubles per year (1989) and that, on the other hand, the standard of living of the smaller, western republics is higher than it is in the Russian Federation (RSFSR). But such differences exist in virtually every country, and it is customary that the richer regions support the poorer ones.

Some spokesmen of the right, such as the writer Rasputin, have threatened that the RSFSR might leave the Soviet Union if the separatist forces among the other nationalities continue to press their demands. But the threat hardly has been meant seriously; most of those on the right believe with Fyodor Dostoevsky in the world historical mission of a Greater Russia. The Russian right may ultimately accept this, but it cannot advocate the liquidation of the empire, just as the British and French conservatives could not have advocated a Little Britain or a Little France. The Russian Federation most likely will be given a greater measure of cultural autonomy and probably also some more administrative autonomy. A Soviet government gravitating more to the right could reduce rock music broadcasts on radio and television, and it might remove liberal and Jewish editors and filmmakers and introduce stronger discipline (party and nationalist) in various fields on the pattern of Brezhnev and Mikhail Suslov. But it still would have no plan for major systemic change. And even if it had such a plan, it would not be in a position to carry it out.

Spokesmen of the advocates of reform speculated from an early date how much time they had to achieve tangible results. The general assumption was that *perestroika* would be in trouble unless they could show substantial achievements within a year or two. However, public opinion polls, for what they are worth, reflected a more complex picture. Less than one third of those polled expected improvement in the near future. If expectations were not high, it stood to reason that the political situation was less immediately critical—unless there were a significant deterioration in the supply situation.

Liberal Apprehensions

The advocates of economic reform no more agreed among themselves than did the right-wing critics of *perestroika*. The consensus was that a self-regulating market was greatly preferable to a rigid planned economy. Nor were they greatly bothered by accusations that this position constituted a retreat from socialist principles. They had no answer to the question of how to accomplish the transition from one system to another, and they clearly underrated in the beginning the enormous difficulties facing them. They underrated the opposition of the bureaucracy as much as they did the inertia of the population at large. They assumed that, since the prevailing system in agriculture was universally loathed, the peasants would warmly welcome the opportunity to rent land and that as a result productivity would sharply rise. They also assumed that city dwellers exasperated by queuing for insufficient supplies of shoddy goods would be only too willing to pay more for higher quality goods. The reformers overestimated the desire of the population to be free of bureaucratic shackles. Everyone cursed the bureaucracy, but their resentment was counterbalanced by a deep, egalitarian bias: "Why should others—for whatever reason—live better than we do?" The reformers assumed that, once the bureaucratic shackles were removed, a spirit of enterprise and initiative would manifest itself, goods would be produced, and services would be provided without constant regulations and commands from above.

By the summer of 1989, at the latest, it was clear that these assumptions had been mistaken. Some argued that, given the pervasive inertia and resistance, a true economic revolution could be carried out only *in extremis,* after a further deterioration in the situation and after it became apparent that there could be no further muddling through and that the alternative was not neo-Brezhnevism but chaos and ruin.[5] Russian history provides more than one example of a supreme effort being made at the last line of retreat, but in some instances the last-minute miracles did not happen. Others who examined the lessons of the past argued that all previous economic reforms had failed because they had not gone far enough and were not accompanied by democratic reforms. The dead hand of the bureaucracy could be overcome only by radical democratization. This is an attractive scenario, but it is based on the assumption that the masses hate the bureaucracy more than they hate the cooperatives, a supposition that cannot be taken for granted. An alternative line of argument was that the bureaucracy was so deeply ingrained in the system that reforms could be accomplished only by a revolution from above: This has been the rule in Russian history.

But was the bureaucracy the only enemy of reform? Is it not true that an enormous amount of disturbance has been caused (and more will be caused) by the masses bursting into politics while lacking democratic convictions and traditions? According to some reformist thinkers to whose views we shall return later on, the masses lack the competence to act in accordance with their own long-term best interests. An abrupt transition from totalitarianism to democracy might well result in chaos, in struggle among narrow group interests, national and social, without any higher authority to provide cohesion by imposing compromises when necessary. For this reason, some called for a temporary dictatorship, preferably of a trusted individual such as Gorbachev, a one-man committee of national salvation rather than the collective leadership of the "partocracy."

Seen from this perspective, the situation was critical: The early years of *perestroika* had been wasted with all kinds of uncoordinated half-measures. The elections and the work of the new Soviet parliament were futile, a waste of time and effort. The

---

[5]P. Bunich, *Argumenty i Fakty*, 38, 1989.

parliament was too slow, and from its debates nothing of great importance had emerged, such as a market. Strong-arm measures were needed to effect truly radical changes.

What these strong-arm reformists had in mind was not so much a return to Caesarism as something akin to the dictatorship practiced in early Roman history, with leading citizens appointed in a time of supreme danger to accomplish specific missions and with certain safeguards (such as *provocatio*, the right to appeal).

Other reformists rejected the iron-fist model as incongruent with the prevailing attitudes and the balance of power in the Soviet Union. A great many voices could be heard warning against dictatorship, but it was by no means certain that these constituted a majority. It was even less certain that these would not fall silent if the situation deteriorated.

The task ahead, as the iron-fist reformists saw it, would take, not a year or two, but decades. Did they favor a liberal dictatorship for this long era of transition, or for just until the end of 1990? This was the period regarded by Academician Leonid Abalkin (an economist and deputy prime minister) as absolutely critical. Or were they merely willing to give Gorbachev, as he demanded, a free hand for the next four years?

The opponents of the iron-fist reformers argued that theirs was a counsel of fear, voiced by people walking along the edge of an abyss without the benefit of a compass. There could be no compass, for the Soviet situation was and is unique. References to Oliver Cromwell, to Napoleon, and even to contemporary Hungary and Poland were not apposite. In Poland, democratic reforms were the result of pressure from below; in Hungary, it was the initiative of the party leadership which proved to be decisive. Neither scenario seems likely in the Soviet Union, certainly not in the short run.

The outlook of the Soviet liberals runs the gamut from utter despair to belief that the situation will improve in the long run, that a more or less stable and democratic system eventually will emerge. Those who believe that the system is not reformable point to the Spanish precedent; Spain under Francisco Franco was a dictatorship, but in contrast to the Soviet Union it was not a totalitarian system. There was no state party, and underneath the surface all kind of power centers existed all along, making possible the relatively smooth and painless transition from military dictatorship to democracy.

In the Soviet Union, on the other hand, such a transition seems impossible because of the immense power of the state and party apparatus and the resistance of the Communist party against power sharing. Without the emergence of a multiparty system there can be no lasting change, and a democratic rebirth would be possible only after a purgatory of a great deal of unrest. However, as long as the power of the state and party apparatus remains unbroken, mass unrest such as strikes and national strife is bound to lead to repression, which might well come in the form of a military coup. This apparent lack of any remedy, peaceful or violent, is the cause of the feeling of doom among not a few members of the "democratic party."

The circumstances in which a coup could occur were widely discussed a quarter of a century after Khrushchev was overthrown. Could it happen again? Many reformers thought it was possible, indeed likely, because (as one of them put it) in no other country was the ruling class so afraid for its skin, so unwilling to give up any of its privileges as was the *nomenklatura.* Such allegations were rejected by military spokesmen (for instance, by Marshal Sergei Akhromeyev) as deeply insulting. Whenever the army had taken action, as in the case of Beria's arrest in 1953, it had been on the orders of the political leadership. Even some leading spokesmen of the opposition to present CPSU leadership such as Yeltsin argued that a coup was a practical impossibility, either for military leaders or for individual members of the Politburo.[6]

These predictions did not reassure the democrats. A situation could still arise, as the late Andrei Sakharov put it in an interview, in which "we no longer care whether Gorbachev is in power or

---

[6]*Argumenty i Fakty,* 27, 1989.

not." What if Gorbachev reneged on his liberal promises, what if part of the political leadership plotted against the rest, what if the general situation deteriorated and the conviction grew that a return to a state-of-siege system was imperative? Since the army commanders and the KGB were not in the forefront of the struggle for liberty but instead regarded themselves almost by definition as the main bulwark against chaos, anarchy, and nihilism, a coup—sudden and violent, or quite legal—could by no means be excluded. At best a coup would lead to the muzzling of the democratic forces, at worst to a wholesale pogrom directed against the advocates of freedom.

Many observers of the Soviet scene argued that the longer the country had known some degree of freedom, the more the masses had been politicized, the more difficult it would be to turn the wheel back. Much was made of the fact that, in many respects, dual power *(dvoevlastie)* had already come into being, as it had before the revolution of October 1917. But there was one essential difference: The whole party-state-security apparatus was now intact.

It is true that the long-term perspective even of leading members of the *nomenklatura* was not War Communism (1918–1920) or Brezhnevism but a system, broadly speaking, similar to Scandinavian social democracy. But, since the Scandinavian model was beyond reach, there seemed to be in an emergency no alternative but a return to a dictatorial regime.

A new authoritarian system could take a variety of forms, including a relatively permissive civilian dictatorship in which some dissent would be permitted, provided it did not undermine the regime or result in substantial political change. But it could also appear as a harsh dictatorship in which all legal niceties again would be suspended.

What could a new authoritarianism achieve, and how long would it be likely to last? Any significant economic progress seems unlikely under such auspices, but the system still could have a measure of popular support if it appeared to be the only alternative to chaos. The military-party dictatorship in Poland lasted for seven years, but the Polish example is not a guidepost. Poland faced tremendous economic difficulties, but it was ethnically homogenous, whereas the Soviet Union confronts separatist movements, which complicate the situation and make democratization more difficult. True, the Soviet Union may become more homogenous as the result of the secession of various republics. But the mood in such a country, a postimperialist RSFSR, will more likely be one of resentment than of democratic zest and reformist ardor, at least for a considerable period.

Alexis de Tocqueville once wrote that democratic nations are haunted by visions of what will be: "In this direction their unbounded imagination grows and dilates beyond all measure." As far as its preoccupation with the future is concerned, the Soviet Union certainly has moved closer to a democratic mentality, and with good reason, for never were the stakes so high and the future so uncertain.

•3•
THE FUTURE OF ECONOMIC REFORM

Gur Ofer

The Future of Economic Reform: An Overview

RADICAL ECONOMIC REFORMS have been forced on the Soviet Union by declining growth rates that started some twenty years ago and reached virtual stagnation during the early 1980s. The per capita GNP of the Soviet economy is only about 40 percent (or less) of that of the United States and other highly developed countries. Worse yet, most analysts, both in the West and in the Soviet Union, maintain that the decline and stagnation represent a long-term trend, not a temporary crisis. The stagnation stems from exhaustion of the growth strategy that has been followed so far, from systemic technological weakness, from the increasing and cumulative inefficiencies of a centrally planned command socialist system, and from the prolonged, intense burden of defense and other "empire"-related expenditures. The input-intensive growth strategy (the so-called extensive growth model) has run its course. The overall productivity of the Soviet economy has

83

been estimated at near-zero or negative levels since 1971. The current strategy must be replaced by an intensive growth strategy based on growth in productivity growth. The failure to generate productivity growth, in the form of indigenous or even borrowed technological changes, is the most serious weakness of the present system. Both the strategy and the system need to be radically transformed.

Few countries tolerate stagnation, especially at such a low absolute and relative level. The Soviet Union, with a world-power position and responsibilities, is not expected to tolerate stagnation, particularly following more than seventy years of promises to its people to catch up and overtake capitalism. Until recently, most observers held the view that the main goal of the Soviet leadership was to maximize external and internal power building through the maximum development of heavy industry and defense production. They also believed that the welfare of the population was either an intermediate good (under Stalin) or a secondary goal (since Khrushchev). The decline in growth rates experienced by the Soviet Union, as well as its underlying technological weakness, has seriously compromised the country's ability to pursue its traditional goal of building its military capability. A military burden of 15 to 17 percent of GNP, the lowest figure in the range of available estimates, contributes to a declining rate of growth and thus undermines the ability to sustain the arms race. In this respect, the emphasis on military power is self-defeating.

The new Soviet leadership understands this connection and seems to put a higher value than has been done in the past on economic capability as an element of both internal and external power. This should shift the direction of leadership efforts toward economic reform and, at least to some extent, away from the military.

Most observers now accept that, since 1985, Mikhail Gorbachev has put forward a different set of goals for the Soviet Union. Raising the economic welfare of the population has moved to a much higher position of importance, if not the top position. Gorbachev is fully convinced that he will not be able to resume growth and increase the standard of living of the Soviet population without a significant cut in the rate of growth of defense expenditures. This is the motivation for his new foreign defense policies aimed at diffusing conflicts at all levels, improving international cooperation, drastically cutting existing stockpiles of arms, and limiting the arms race. I fully agree with this estimate and cannot foresee sustained economic growth, let alone an improvement in the population's welfare, without a radical reform of the system and a considerable shift in resource allocation away from the military. These two sets of changes interact, but for the purpose of this section let us initially separate the two into distinct discussions. The ongoing economic reform through the end of the century can be discussed with little or no reference to the size of the military budget. But the economic reforms may enable the Soviet Union to expand or improve its military capabilities. The apprehension that this may be the case and that the current shift toward détente may grant the Soviets a much-needed breathing spell, as well as the use of Western credits and technology to regain economic and military capabilities, is one of the arguments against Western support for the reforms.

The Prospects of Economic Reform

AN ASSESSMENT OF THE SOVIET REFORM

The main difference between the present wave of reforms in the Soviet Union and all previous attempts is the wide range of currently proposed actions. They encompass changes in the economic, political, social, cultural, and ideological spheres of life. It has been stated many times that the additional changes are needed for the success of economic reform. This is an important innovation: Until recently, the Soviet leadership held that isolated economic reforms were possible and that no political or cultural changes were needed or would be tolerated. At times even some Western Sovietologists, watching the fast rate of economic growth in the Soviet Union in the past, doubted whether political, social, and personal freedoms were indeed necessary for economic modernization. Now, we have it on the authority of the general secretary that the wider reforms are essential. What is now happening in the Soviet Union is still very far from the Western concept of a democratic society, or even of a civil society. It is, however, a clear first step in this direction, and, however small, it is truly revolutionary in Soviet terms. In the short run, Gorbachev is using *glasnost* and political reform to generate support in his struggle for economic reform and for other changes, and so far the impact of the reforms has been mostly positive. In the long run, these reforms are an integral part of Gorbachev's vision of a new Soviet society. The economic reforms range widely, encompassing all sectors of the economy and covering almost every aspect of the present economic system.

The core of the economic system—the main manufacturing complex plus transportation, construction, the planning and supply organs, the banks, and other elements—is to remain in the hands of the state, but management by administration will give way to management by economic leverages. Central planning will be replaced by nonbinding planning, to be implemented with the help of an extremely reduced bureaucracy. State procurement orders eventually will cover only a small proportion of total production. (They were said to be down to 20 percent, on average, early in 1989.) The government will also maintain responsibility for important investment projects. Enterprises will be independent, fully accountable, and self-financing—that is, operating under hard budget constraints. They will shape their own production plans, hire labor under a market system, determine their own wage scales (within set boundaries), and engage in voluntary wholesale trade for procurement of supplies and marketing of products.

Prices will be revised first to conform to scarcities and real costs, but later their determination will be largely liberalized and determined, within boundaries and with a number of exceptions, by the market. Enterprises will have to finance investment from profits, by seeking bank credits, or by issuing "shares." Someday they will also be able to engage freely in foreign trade. Enterprises will be allowed not only to make and keep profits, but also to fail and go bankrupt. Special arrangements will be made to avoid unemployment. One exception to a general move toward a market economy is that managers will be elected by the work force of each enterprise.

Macrofiscal and monetary policies will become the major regulatory tools of the government to ensure monetary stability and fiscal responsibility. A host of financial institutions will be established or reformed in order to provide credit for both working capital and long-term investments and to enforce the hard budget constraints on enterprises. Balanced monetary and credit policies will be used to avoid inflation. Enterprises will deal with banks in a market-like fashion.

This sounds like a conversion to a market economy, but most of it is still on paper. The balance between government orders and wholesale trade is as yet centrally determined, and the true meaning of many of the terms used, such as "contract," "voluntary," "indicative," and "hard," are unknown. Their definition will determine the final nature of the reform and its chances to succeed.

An urban private and cooperative sector is to be established. The private enterprises will be limited to self-employed people who do not have to work in the public sector and to after-hours work. What is more significant, cooperatives will be permitted to operate like the state enterprises and employ workers. The private sector is designed mostly to provide services but enterprises can be established in every sphere, including manufacturing, transport, construction, and trade. In addition, government enterprises or sections of government enterprises may be leased out to cooperatives. A capital market of sorts will be developed in which workers of a given enterprise, government enterprise, or cooperative will be able to purchase and trade "shares" of other enterprises. In this way, substantial parts of the core economy will have quasi- and fully-privately owned enterprises.

If it were fully developed, such a private sector clearly could help to revamp the retarded service sector and create competition both with and within the state sector. It would relieve the planning authorities from the impossible task of planning and managing all services.

The radical reform of agriculture is still to be formulated. (In place already are the abolition of central planning and some relaxation of obligatory deliveries to the state. Farms are allowed to sell in private markets.) Eventually there will be free trade. Private plots are encouraged as are short-term leases and collective contracts whereby groups of farmers unite under contract to produce for the farm (state or collective) or to lease land and equipment to produce on their own. The main reform programs that have been advanced by the Soviet leadership are long-term (forty-nine-year) leases (and a possible return to private farming). The role of the collective farm is envisaged as providing supplies and financial and professional services to individual farmers or private cooperatives, which will play a role similar to that of Western agricultural cooperatives. The doctrinal legitimacy of types of property relations different from state or *kolkhoz* ownership in agriculture has been reestablished. This could amount to virtual decollectivization, similar to the Chinese pattern, and to a return of the "farmer" as the preferred caretaker of the land. He is expected to replace the collective farmer, who is blamed for inefficiencies of agricultural production and is derogatively called a "day worker."

Reforms in foreign economic relations include two main elements. The first is the liberalization of foreign trade. Already, the foreign trade monopoly has been abolished, and, under strict regulations, the right to trade has been granted to ministries and large enterprises. The long-term goal is to continue liberalization until every enterprise is permitted to trade: first, under regulation and, eventually, with a convertible ruble. This will take a long time, but the goal is set. The second element is the sanction of foreign investment in the Soviet Union in the form of joint ventures, although restrictions on expatriating profits remain in force. Judging by its pace up until now, liberalization is bound to continue. Special economic zones and other initiatives are being considered to expedite the opening of the Soviet economy.

Opening the Soviet economy to both competition and investment is one of the most potentially significant reforms. The lack of competition and the weakness in technology are among the main contributors to the economy's low level of efficiency. These changes, however, can be productive only following internal reforms of the kind described, which are needed to attract and facilitate the external activity.

Another key reform is a long-range shift in resources from defense and investment to consumption. Gorbachev's modernization plan is to produce much higher quality machines and equipment, retool existing plants, retire obsolete equipment, and eliminate unnecessary investment in construction. In order to achieve quick results, this program has been run as a high-priority, mission-oriented effort. During the first few years, it has demanded more investment outlays, causing a postponement in the diversion of resources to the consumer sector. In the future, more investment will be directed to service links, such as storage, transportation, and trade, and less to direct production to compensate for a long period of neglect of these supposedly less-essential or even nonproductive spheres.

Finally, there is a call for more emphasis on quality instead of on the long-standing quantity targets, which have been damaging. This change should come mostly as a result of other reforms. Until they take hold, special administrative means are to be employed to raise the quality of goods. Unfortunately, quantity targets have not been reduced as part of the routine of showing results.

On paper, given the right interpretation, the main elements of the reforms look very impressive. Using the experience of the mixed, but quite highly regulated, economies in the West, this conceivably could be a blueprint for a considerably better performance than that of today's Soviet economy. Assuming a more radical interpretation of the reforms and of the meaning of the terms used, there should be enough competition, market forces, personal incentives, and flexibility to provide an adequate environment for sustained growth.

The economic reality in the Soviet Union at the present time, however, is far removed from this vision, and, in a number of aspects, its performance is even worse than that of the old system. Many people who judge the reforms on the basis of the present situation come up with very pessimistic verdicts. The present disorder, confusion, contradictions, and setbacks may signal failure, but alternatively they may attest to the inevitable struggle with transition. In order to arrive at a reasonable judgement, however, one has to understand the dynamics of reform under the current circumstances.

THE DYNAMICS OF REFORM

One can envision four different concepts or ranges of change in the context of Gorbachev's reform. The first is change against one of the most rigid, change-proof systems in the world. From this perspective, any change at all, however small and insignificant, can be considered revolutionary. The early, small stages of Soviet reforms, back in 1985, were surely considered revolutionary. That revolutionary changes are difficult to conceive, accept, and gain consensus for places a very severe constraint upon how far or fast one can move at the beginning. As time goes on, and more changes are introduced, the psychological barriers against more radical change decline.

Another concept of change focuses on the minimum changes needed to transform the Soviet economy into a viable, growing system. Some economists, such as Nikolai Shmelyov and Leonid Abalkin, advocate a drastic shift in the direction of a market system based on competition, with only a minimum of administrative intervention. These would be truly revolutionary changes from every viewpoint—economic, political, social, psychological, and ideological. The critical "minimum" needed to effect the transformation is not at all clear, nor is it clear how to get there; what is clear is that the needed changes go much beyond what the political leaders have been able or willing to consider feasible, at least at the beginning. These economists are pushing not only for the most radical reforms but also to implement them quickly and as an internally consistent package.

Between these two extreme perspectives is that of the political reformers, led by Gorbachev, who are pushing for reforms but are more conservative and cautious than are the economists. Gorbachev at first seemed to believe that it should be possible to turn the economy around with less marketization and competition, less privatization, less surrender of state control, and fewer doctrinal concessions than were demanded by the economists. Over time, however, Gorbachev realized that the deficiencies of the old system were much worse than he had assumed at the outset. His views on what constitutes the minimum necessary reform have evolved in favor of more radical changes. Recent pronouncements seem to indicate that he is willing to travel almost any distance to ensure that the turnabout will happen. He has been cautious, however, in order to avoid too much resistance and, therefore, has yet to paint the entire picture in great detail in the form of operational programs.

The fourth perspective on change follows the actual execution of reforms. From the economic point of view, a single consistent package of changes has a better chance of success, although results may show up only after a long transitional period and many hardships. Such a plan may have a greater risk of political abortion in midstream. The alternative is a more gradual economic reform with less painful and possibly quicker results, albeit superficial ones, with higher chances of political acceptance. The risk is that contradictions created by partial changes in the economic system will cause disenchantment with the reform. In the beginning, when Gorbachev's envisaged reform was not considered radical, its execution difficulties were underestimated. It was assumed that the economy still had enough reserves to ward off any catastrophe, and plans were drawn for a relatively quick shift, as manifested in the ambitious twelfth five-year plan. But during the first three years of the plan it became clear that these reserves did not exist, that the initial economic situation was much worse than had been assumed, and that the efficiency improvements expected from the discipline drive and the antialcohol campaign were disappointing. Instead, there were strong inertia and a very slow response to change, and a great many mistakes were made. Finally, serious political and ideological opposition developed. The leadership was forced to accept political compromises, to slow down the pace of the reform, and to accept partial economic steps with limited internal logic.

There are, apparently, two conflicting dynamic trends inside the leadership group of Gorbachev and his close advisers. There is a growing realization that the reforms will have to go much further than was initially assumed, but there also is a growing recognition that the execution of the reforms will be much rougher and will need to be stretched out over a longer period of time than was anticipated. This gap has been described as a growing cleavage between Gorbachevism as a reform and Gorbachev as a politician.

Although there is a determination to move ahead with the reforms, and although some of the psychological barriers are becoming softer over time, political and social considerations and compromises will probably hold back the pace of the economic reform. Reform will continue to proceed gradually with partial measures taken one at a time. Economic reform measures will not necessarily follow a rational order and will continue to lack internal consistency, in order to be politically and socially feasible. As it was during the first three years of the reform, this approach will reduce the effectiveness of many of the steps taken as well as their economic benefits to the population.

Such half-measures also raise doubts regarding the effectiveness of the reform and may even instigate countermeasures that will push the reforms backward. Examples abound. Many observers have criticized Gorbachev for not starting with reforms in agriculture, in which the potential payoff would be high, both in terms of raising production and raising the consumption level of the population, thereby creating the right atmosphere for further, perhaps more painful reforms. One explanation for this decision is certainly the very high ideological cost of denouncing collectivization and sixty years of agricultural policies. Another example of a half-measure is the granting of independence to most enterprises to make their own plans and to shift to self-financing without also creating independent trade networks and without reforming prices. Even the very limited pricing freedom granted to enterprises has created a general outcry over inflation and over the disappearance of basic goods from the marketplace. The outcry has prompted administrative countermeasures, the worst that could happen to the reform. Of course, one cannot let go of prices before the fiscal and monetary systems are prepared. But these preparations are conditioned upon closing the huge government budget deficit, which in turn involves reducing state subsidies for basic foods and other consumer goods, the most sensitive political issue of all.

Another partial measure is the legislation allowing private and cooperative activities. The hesitation in enacting far-reaching and clear legislation caused a very slow start of cooperative activities, which in turn produced very high prices initially. The public outcry triggered countermeasures, again mostly administrative, which held back the development of this very important sector. A more generous approach at the outset could have allowed a much wider and quicker development of the sector, with lower initial prices and more public acceptance. Because there is no theory for the transition, hesitation here, as elsewhere, reflects in addition to ideological, social, and political factors, a lack of confidence and plain policy mistakes.

The internal logic of the sequence of reform steps combines political, social, ideological, and economic considerations. This logic, or lack thereof, includes contradictions that entail a considerable price and raise the risk of economic failure. The overall balancing act attempts to compensate for the losses so as to make the reform process feasible. Gorbachev, either by choice or by political necessity, has followed a gradual, little-of-everything reform plan. This is one reason for the very meager economic results so far and the general malaise in the economic sector. The gradual approach is a major impediment to full economic reform, but there are many others.

MAIN OBSTACLES AND BOTTLENECKS

Economic reforms were announced only when the old development strategy had reached the end of its rope, when there was no other choice but to seek change. When previous leaders faced the difficult reform option in 1964, but could choose whether to proceed with or without it, they took the line of least resistance. On the one hand, having no choice could have been the greatest advantage for the reforms' success and a source of strength against conservative opposition. On the other hand, last-minute action meant entering a prolonged period of reforms with few of the reserves that are essential to bridge a temporary crisis or to be able to pay up front, thereby inducing the population to increase its efforts and support for the reforms before the reforms themselves bear any results.

As it turned out, the economic situation at the outset was even worse than could be discerned from statistics. For a long time before the crisis the Soviet economy had managed to proceed, albeit with declining growth rates, only by accumulating heavy debt, by mortgaging its future. This debt was incurred not in external loans but rather by using up the country's natural and human resources at rates that were much faster than was economically warranted. These "loans" also took the form of underdevelopment and disregard for the physical infrastructure needed to sustain long-term development. This infrastructure includes the transportation system, storage and distribution systems, communications, urban infrastructure, and many subsidiary production processes.

To a point, production could proceed by stretching the poor infrastructure beyond its limits and by using expensive stopgap improvisations, but over time this neglect caused more and more bottlenecks and inhibited economic efficiency. Gorbachev was forced to invest massively in infrastructure of all kinds to replace much of the obsolete production capital that had been kept in place to ensure meeting production demands. The traditional Soviet model of growth was characterized by haste, by a willingness to mortgage future prospects for short-term gains, and by continuously growing future losses per each ruble of present gains. The essence of Gorbachev's economic reform has been to eliminate haste, to relieve pressure for mere quantitative results, and to create enough room to allow quality improvement and technological change. Still, the economy has been burdened by the large amount of remaining "interest" payments and loan repayments left over from the old regime.

The chief obstacle to reform is the general fear of change. For many years, the economic system operated under a constant pressure to produce more and more to meet ever-increasing production demands. These pressures, along with the perennial shortages and the rigidly hierarchical administrative system, forced enterprises to stick to established production and supply patterns. Introduction of any innovations in production or supply risked unfulfilled plans. Most of the partial reforms that were introduced over the years were circumvented or "simulated," in one way or another, so as to avoid making any significant changes. The risks involved always outweighed the usually short-lived rewards. Better performance during a given year caused increased production demands for the following one. Most efforts to encourage technological change failed, as did efforts to encourage enterprises to work with hard budget constraints. The same was true at the administrative level: All efforts over the years to grant enterprises more freedom of action were made futile by the pressure on the lower administration levels to come up with the expected production results.

There is serious danger that new reforms will suffer the same fate or at least will take too long for real change to take hold. The danger is that the new "indicative" plan will simply become the old obligatory plan, "contract" will become synonymous with "state order," and "full accountability"—a term invented to indicate that enterprises are responsible for their finances—will eventually revert to simple accountability. Enterprises will continue to buy from the old suppliers and sell to the same stores, and low-level bureaucrats, fearful as ever of failing to meet their "indicative" quotas, will continue their tutelage, and bonuses will continue to be paid routinely. There are many signs that this is already happening, including Gorbachev's persistent complaints. The danger will be even greater if production does not increase, if prices do not change, and if shortages persist. It is a vicious circle.

Inertia and fear of change are strengthened by the fact that the Soviet economic reform is a revolution from above, with no particular social or economic class pushing for it. If such a class existed, it would have developed a favorable balance (at least for itself) of risks and rewards for change. The success or failure of the change would be determined by its ability to convince the rest of society to comply. Although almost all classes and most individuals would gain much from the reform's success, most groups shy away from taking any extra efforts or risks for highly questionable rewards in the uncertain future. Soviet citizens are accustomed to waiting, often in vain, for the fruits of their efforts to show up in the distant future. It is very difficult to convince them that the rules of the game have changed. This is why early results are so important. Although a revolution from above has obvious advantages, it still depends upon the faith of the people that the revolution is working.

A related obstacle facing this revolution is that the governing elite, both party and administrative, with perhaps the exception of the very top, has to relinquish much of its power and privileges. This problem becomes more and more acute as one goes down the hierarchy: The identification with the general goals of the reform declines, as does the chance of preserving one's job should the changes be made. It is difficult to obtain the participation of middle- and low-level bureaucrats in preparing new legislation or regulations, and more so in enforcing them, because it is very difficult to force these people to work against their own interests.

Considering the new independent status planned for state enterprise managers and the important role assigned to the private sector, both rural and urban, the question arises of whether there will be enough entrepreneurs to take advantage of the new conditions. The standard response of economists is that, if the right environment has been created, the potential entrepreneurs will be waiting. There are, however, those who doubt that this will be the case following seventy years of socialist rule preceded by the mere beginning of capitalist development. The question is raised with special concern about agriculture. Even if there is no shortage of dormant entrepreneurial energy, its full manifestation in the economy will be delayed by lack of training, by ideological hang-ups, and by the probably slow pace of the creation of a market.

Many of the conditions that are required to facilitate competition and the operation of a market system are unfulfilled. The first, basic condition, and the most difficult one to attain, is the need to develop an intrinsic understanding of these elusive concepts. In a country that has never taught Western market economics, and has always believed in direct intervention, it is very difficult to internalize the concept of the "invisible hand." There is a real danger that the market will continue to be considered something anarchical which constantly needs to be tamed. One of the most serious dangers is that, instead of letting a badly functioning limited market correct itself by expansion or by the relaxation of unnecessary regulations, the market will be limited further or even stifled by too much regulation. This happens sometimes in the Western market economies, and it is easy to see how this could create a prolonged barrier for reform in the Soviet Union. Under such circumstances, overregulation and control could lead to an incorrect diagnosis regarding the absence of entrepreneurship.

Markets need prices that are correct and responsive to market forces. At present, prices in the Soviet Union are both wrong and fixed by the state. The process of revising prices to conform more or less to costs, which is planned as a first step, and of devising a method by which prices will then be allowed to move, will be difficult and protracted. Price reform will require coordination with fiscal, monetary, and social policies, and there is bound to be error along the way.

An additional obstacle to the creation of a market environment is the present structure of Soviet industry. It is highly concentrated and monopolistic, and the markets for inputs and products are strictly segmented. Enterprises have permanent suppliers, and they sell in restricted local markets. Breaking up monopolies and meshing supply and trade markets will be a prolonged process. It is undesirable to let prices go loose before competition is ensured.

The shift from a system based on administrative means to one based on economic means demands a parallel shift of the entire macroeconomic infrastructure. First, the planning and control system must be replaced by sound monetary and fiscal systems, which were of secondary importance under central planning. Under the present system there is a limited role for the monetary system and the money supply: Too much money in the hands of the population creates lines and repressed inflation, but up to a point this surplus is functional, for it ensures that almost all that is produced for consumption will be purchased.

The production sector is almost completely isolated from the general monetary system. It operates on the basis of unconnected credit and debit balances for the major inputs and products. For example, increasing the wage fund credit to an enterprise, beyond the planned amount, so as to ensure production plan fulfillment, is a very common practice. Similarly, government deficits often are created to provide for defense or other needs. Eventually too much money and the accumulation of unwanted savings affect work and enterprise incentives, creating shortages and demoralization. Before one moves to create markets, to free prices, or to open the economy, market-type monetary and fiscal systems must be established, after the resolution of old monetary excesses. A significant part of the present excess actually has been created during the reform period, stemming from the decline in tax revenues from alcohol sales and the partial liberalization of wage payments and bank credits. For the first time, open inflation has started to develop. When one accounts for a current budget deficit of up to 100 billion rubles (about 11 percent of the GNP), a monetary hangover equal to at least a full year of total private consumption, the lack of a market-type banking system, and the need to overhaul the system to service the growing private sector, one can envisage a long and complicated process before the system becomes stable and the fear of inflation abates. The alternative—tolerating high rates of price increases, which will be very difficult to stop—is politically unacceptable and economically disruptive.

In addition, reform requires an overhauled or even newly created legal system. There is a need not only to write many new laws, but also to establish a completely new legal code of behavior, one in which laws matter and are binding. The present status of the cooperatives and new joint ventures underlines both needs. Also, there is a need to totally reform the statistical reporting system. New curricula in economics and business should be developed, and educational institutions should be renewed. Finally, there is a need to develop, almost from scratch, a new infrastructure of trade, marketing, and business services.

A very high hurdle to be negotiated is the opening up of the Soviet economy and its eventual integration in the world market. This can start seriously only after the basic internal market system is in place, after a suitable infrastructure of services is created. The Soviet Union faces an uphill effort in introducing its manufactures into the world market. Its technology is not only inferior but also, in many cases incompatible with Western standards. It lacks marketing, financing, and servicing experience, and the development of its industrial structure has been oriented all along toward internal needs. The disastrous condition of agriculture precludes exports. The low priority extended to consumer manufactures and to services will deny the Soviet Union the opportunity to penetrate those markets in the foreseeable future. Soviet producers must compete with the most advanced countries, and the Soviet Union is particularly behind in high-tech electronics and information equipment. Finally, any effort to export manufactures during the coming decade and beyond will be challenged by competition from the newly industrialized countries in Asia, Latin America, and southern Europe.

Finally, there is one most difficult barrier to cross—the development of indigenous technology. This is the main goal of the entire reform effort, designed to make possible sustained and intensive growth. At present, the Soviet civilian R&D effort is in very poor shape, squeezed by the inhospitable centrally planned environment and by the encroachments of its military counterpart. At present, imports of advanced Western technology are few, and it is not widely diffused. Economic reforms call for a shift in R&D institutions from ministerial or government budgeting to self-financing by joining enterprises or by seeking contracts from enterprises. In view of the difficulties that face the enterprises during the transition period, and efforts by these enterprises to stay within their means, R&D efforts may initially decline, with improvement expected only in the more distant future.

To the above list of economic difficulties and requirements should be added the fact that there is neither an established theory, nor much experience, on how to move from a centrally planned to a market-oriented system. Many mistakes are bound to be made. The economic program cannot proceed according to its own logic and requirements. It must take into account politics, ideology, and social considerations.

At the minimum, the process of reform will be a very long one, extending beyond the present century. There will be ups and downs and more than one crisis, and positive results will come very slowly and in small doses. Indeed, reform may fail completely at an early stage. The expected gains in productivity in many cases will be offset by mistakes. A disproportionate share of any production increases will have to be directed toward investment in modernization and in infrastructure. The consumer, the main target of the reform and very likely one of its weakest links, will have to wait much longer than was initially assumed.

The Communist leaders will hesitate. If it is successful, the reform will bring about a drastic decline in the power of the

Communist party and most of its officials as well as many government bureaucrats. Gorbachev and some of his closest associates are ready to travel a great distance away from some of the cornerstones of the Soviet socialist system, including state ownership of the means of production, collectivization, and denial of privately earned profits and of privately employed workers. There long has been a great deal of cynicism among the population. There also has been cynicism inside the elite about doctrine and ideology. In great measure, this has been a reaction to the hypocritical behavior of members of the elite, manifested in privileges, corruption, and self-serving behavior. At least some of the opposition to reform measures, especially at high levels, must be explained by the wish to protect power positions; only in part is it motivated by doctrinal conservatism.

Beyond this, across wide parts of the Soviet society there is strong support for equality or fairness in income distribution and for social justice, and strong resistance against people who make a lot of money, especially if it is gained through unearned income. The distinction between "earned" and "unearned" income is not always clear, but unearned income is concentrated especially in trade, financial services, interest, profits, rents, and personal services, particularly when prices seem to be much higher than the material costs of production. Gorbachev has put much effort into fighting for what he terms "leveling" of wages or income without regard for productivity (here, he stands on firm Marxist ground)—a testimony to the strength of the social conviction regarding this norm. This deeply entrenched belief that trade and services are not really productive has impeded the progress of reform. Initially, prices in and income from newly created markets and cooperative enterprises are bound to be high, because they are established in areas in which shortages are most extreme. High rates of income will attract more business that, in turn, will increase supply and reduce prices. Ideologically based control of these incomes may stop the development of new markets.

Related to the social stand on income is the more general issue of the state's social and welfare policies. At present, one part of the government's income support and redistribution program is integrated into its wage policy, leveling wage differences more than would otherwise occur under a market system. Another part of welfare policy is the large subsidy for basic foodstuffs, other consumer goods, housing, and other services. The new wage policy supports a closer relationship between pay and productivity, and reducing subsidies will cause prices and rents to rise sharply. Both changes are key elements of reform, designed to increase production incentives, help to balance the state budget, reduce artificial shortages, and rationalize the consumer goods markets. Although the state apparently plans to offer low- and medium-income families direct income maintenance programs to compensate for the withdrawn subsidies, there is very strong social and political opposition, especially to price revisions. Low prices for basic needs have assumed a social value of their own, and, in addition, there seems to be little trust in the government's promise to compensate. This strong resistance stands in the way of price reform and of efforts to balance the state budget, two essential prerequisites to many aspects of reform.

Finally, the provisions made by the reforms to allow bankruptcies and layoffs of workers raise the possibility of unemployment. This, even if compensated, is fiercely resisted on ideological and social grounds. Whatever one thinks of the merit of these social positions and values, it is clear that they are going to hold back the advance of the reforms, especially during the early stages when the most extreme resource misallocations will come up for correction, while the compensating social policies, at best, make their first steps.

PROJECTIONS

What is the reasonable range of possible growth rates and changes in the structure of the economy, and, within this range, which variants are more likely to be realized between now and the end of this century? Because we are preoccupied with internal Soviet developments, let us assume that external, global economic conditions for the rest of the century will be reasonably favorable: Although oil prices will not rise significantly, and although competition in the world market may intensify with the increasing involvement of the newly industrialized countries, the general trend in the world economy will be toward moderate growth, with even faster growth of international trade. We further assume that the West will respond in kind to the changes in the Soviet policies; that is, it will go along with further arms reduction and limitation agreements, it will cooperate in efforts to diffuse regional conflict and other sources of tension, it will be willing to provide reasonable amounts of credit and to invest directly in the Soviet Union, and it will even relax some of the restrictions on transfer of technology. We also assume no crisis of major proportions in the Soviet empire.

Past and present macroeconomic models of the Soviet Union are not of much help with projecting Soviet growth. In most cases, no matter how detailed and complicated the models are, economic growth rates depend almost exclusively on the assumed rate of growth of productivity in the economy. This, in turn, cannot be determined by objective means but instead is related in a rather impressionistic way to variants of internal reforms and to changes in external conditions. The uncertainty about the progress of reform transfers to the assumptions about productivity.

Most of the other factors that contribute to economic growth in the Soviet Union are fairly predictable. Seldom do any of the econometric models discover important bottlenecks caused by the shortage of a scientific input. This leaves labor and capital. The rate of growth of labor can usually be estimated with great accuracy, and the rate of growth of capital, which is policy-driven and therefore unstable, turns out to have relatively little effect on the final outcome. Very high investment rates and flawed investment policies result in very low capital productivity.

A typical macroeconomic estimate of future Soviet growth, assuming no rise in productivity, as in the recent past, will produce a rate of growth in the GNP of between 1.5 and 2.0 percent per year. This ceiling on possible growth of the Soviet economy without growth in productivity translates, at best, to a 1 percent growth of consumption per capita. Such a low rate of growth of GNP would imply that both investment and defense, which usually grow faster, would encroach on the share of consumption.

What can be assumed about productivity growth? Every 1 percent growth in productivity contributes 1 percent to the rate of growth of GNP. Productivity growth is the outcome of technological and other changes that help to raise output, given a certain amount of input. Western estimates of productivity growth in the Soviet Union over the past twenty years or so have been consistently very close to zero, or even negative, and indicate a decline over time, including the last five years under Gorbachev. At the other extreme are the estimated productivity growth rates of about 2 to 3 percent per year implied by the fifteen-year plan unveiled by Gorbachev at the end of 1985. They should be considered clearly too optimistic. For comparison, rates of growth of productivity in Western countries range from 1 to 3 percent per year, with higher rates in exceptional cases such as Japan and some Asian newly industrialized countries.

Let us assume that, at the end of a successful transition period of reform lasting from fifteen to twenty years, the Soviet economy will achieve the long-term Western rate of productivity growth of 1.5 percent per year. Under assumptions of less successful trajectories or longer transitional periods, there will be lower outcomes. In addition, in case of successful reforms, one may assume that the Soviet Union will be able to remedy most or all of its deficiency in output due to the inefficiency of its old socialist system and its economic policies as compared with similar market economies. An estimate made by Abram Bergson along these lines produced a Soviet efficiency gap of approximately 30 percent. Such estimates are necessarily very crude; let us assume that over the transitional period, the Soviet Union may gain, at most, an additional 20 percent of efficiency, that is, 1.0 to 1.5 percent per year. Again, under less successful scenarios, the rates will be lower.

Finally, we have to take into account the temporary efficiency loss during the period of reform resulting from mistakes, wrong sequencing, learning, opposition, etc. Based on the record of the first four years of reforms, this offsetting factor may be as large as the entire potential productivity gain from all sources, resulting in zero productivity growth throughout the transition. This will be considered here as the lowest likely estimate, although worse scenarios cannot be ruled out. A more optimistic projection would be that during the transition period one half of the potential productivity will be lost to learning and the rate of loss will be larger at the beginning and decline over time.

ANNUAL RATES OF GROWTH

Scenarios	GNP Growth			Production Growth			Consumption Per Capita		
	Beginning	*End*	*Average**	*Beginning*	*End*	*Average**	*Beginning*	*End*	*Average**
High	1.8	3.3	2.5	0.0	1.5	0.75	1.0	2.5	1.7
Medium	1.8	2.6	2.2	0.0	0.75	0.4	1.0	1.8	1.4
Low	1.8			0.0			1.0		

*Beginning of the period is assumed to be 1989; end of the period is assumed to be between the years 2000–2005; and the average is the resulting rate of growth over the period.

In the most optimistic scenario, GNP growth could go as high as 3.3 percent per year at the end of the transition period and productivity could be as high as 1.5 percent. With 2.5 percent GNP growth per year, Soviet GNP by the end of the century would be about one-third higher than it is at present, without any likely gain relative to the Western countries.

Consumption per capita may go up beyond the above estimates for three reasons. First, development of the private and cooperative sectors is expected to be concentrated mainly in agriculture, services, and the production of consumer goods. If this private activity develops quickly, the consumer sector may advance much faster than the state sector of heavy and large industry, and possibly of defense, not unlike what happened during the NEP years. Second, after a period of heavy investment, it may be possible to reduce the share of gross investment in GNP from more than 30 percent today to about 25 percent—still a large figure by international standards. Over the transitional period, this will free perhaps an additional one-half percentage point of GNP per year altogether. Such a decline in the share of investment is part of Gorbachev's program, and it was incorporated into the twelfth five-year plan, for 1986–1990. The modernization programs and bottlenecks in infrastructure have forced Gorbachev to continue with high investment rates, however, and it is not clear when it will be possible to reduce them. Finally, resources may be transferred from the military budget if its share in the GNP is allowed to decline. It should be emphasized that these potential transfers from investment and defense to consumption would be one-time transfers, they would last only as long as the respective shares of investment and defense were declining, and they would cease when a new, stable distribution of resources was reached. It is important that the planned shifts in resource allocation start as soon as possible. The resulting increased rates of growth of consumption could greatly improve the reform's political prospects and, in addition, could help to raise work incentives, productivity, and, hence, production. The question is whether this is possible.

The Military Civilian Trade-off

The very heavy burden of defense on the Soviet economy can be viewed as another manifestation of the long-term Soviet policy of haste, of rushing forward with a huge military buildup while not only neglecting the economic base needed to support it but actually harming it. The long-term military monopoly over the best resources, especially in machine building and in research and development (R&D), has created a situation in which the civilian sector can not support the expanding needs of the military in a wide range of new technologies and materials. It is beyond the ability of the military to expand its own production and capability to all areas without devastating the economy fatally. The time has come to pay the bill, and it is now realized that curing the economy is required not only for its own sake but also because the future of Soviet military capability is itself in great jeopardy if this is not accomplished. This realization should generate military support, at least in principle, for economic reform. Of critical importance to the reform is the question of how much the military will be willing to give up.

The emerging economic and military crises have forced the Soviet leadership to redefine its goals and seek new means for attaining them, both in the domestic sphere and in the sphere of national security and international relations. These changes have been manifested in a series of policy pronouncements called the "new thinking." The main points are:

1. Security, in contrast to military capability, depends on economic performance as well as on internal cohesiveness and strength, which is linked to the welfare of the people and to the nature of political relations with adversaries.

2. The military burden may be reduced as the result of a new foreign policy directed at better superpower relations, cooperation and mutual trust, and the reduction of global and regional tensions. It is also based on a deideologization of conflict and an acceptance of the legitimacy of the other side's system. The same or an even greater level of security can thus be achieved with less expensive political inputs.

3. Consistent with the above changes, the Soviet Union is adopting a new strategic doctrine of "sufficiency," limiting the mission of its military forces to defense so as to save on costs by eliminating various offensive equipment and units and also to reduce the aggressive image of its strategy. "Sufficiency," or even "reasonable sufficiency," replaces the policy of maximizing defense capabilities, of trying to cover every possible contingency, however unlikely. Defense has come to emphasize the commitment of the Soviet Union to not starting a war.

This policy was announced by Gorbachev in his December 1988 United Nations speech.

4. The same "new thinking" applies also to Soviet policy toward its empire and toward the Third World: The best source of influence is the viability of the Soviet system at home. Generally, aid should be cut or granted on the basis of mutual benefits and cooperation, and aid granted by the North to the South should be directed through international organizations with cooperation among all donors.

These concepts, if fully implemented, should lead eventually to a reduction of up to 50 percent or more in military stocks and budgets, according to some Western and Soviet observers.

One may wonder why a country with such a clear disadvantage in the arms race, due to its smaller economic base and its systematic technological disadvantage, did not discover these less expensive means to protect itself at a much earlier date? Why did it abandon the détente of the early 1970s in favor of costly and aggressive policies? The Soviet Union has followed all along a policy of provoking the United States and the other Western powers into new rounds of arm races by inflating its real military capability behind a screen of absolute secrecy. This behavior, which led to the Cuban missile crisis of the early 1960s, is yet another manifestation of the policy of haste, of trying to score gains in the short run, with a very high price to be paid later on.

One possible explanation for the apparent paradox of past Soviet behavior is that a new military and international strategy can become credible and sustainable only after the Soviet Union has reached military parity with the West and has demonstrated this to its adversaries and to itself. New thinking should emerge only from a base of strength, lest it be interpreted as an indication of weakness. Thus, the historical debate should be directed to the question of whether the Soviet Union has overplayed the role of superpower. Could new thinking not have been attempted fifteen years earlier, at great savings to the economy? This point has been made in the sharp criticism of the present leadership against its predecessors.

Although one tends to regard the newly proclaimed policies as basically sincere and as a real change in the Soviet way of looking at the world, the exact parameters and military implications of the new thinking have not yet been fully defined. Only part of the new policies can be implemented unilaterally; their full test depends on the response of the Western powers. Even with this new thinking, the Soviet Union remains a formidable military power and plans to continue this role well into the future. It is not unilaterally disarming, and it will not give up willingly its position of parity. Although it has declared its intention to reduce some of its most threatening postures, for most technical purposes the threat is still there.

The final element of the new military strategy is a modernization program for Soviet military forces. A sharp reduction in size is to be compensated by an across-the-board upgrading of weapon systems technology, training, and manpower to Western state-of-the-art standards. This modernization plan, involving intensive R&D and production efforts, has become the only aspect of military reform that strongly competes with the economic reforms. The exact size and extent of the modernization program is not yet clear; this may well be a topic requiring hard bargaining between the political leaders, who are eager to stretch it out over a long period of time and to incorporate it as an integral part of the economic reforms, and the military. In view of all the other demands from the military in connection with economic reform, it may well be that the compromise will be closer to the military version of the plan. The modernization plan may also become a source of suspicion in the West and of apprehension about the final destination of any technological assistance that may be granted.

There are various forms of competition and resource trade-off between the military and the civilian sectors. The most general trade-off is in total resources: a larger military GNP share implies less for civilian production. Seventeen percent of GNP for military spending constitutes an exceptionally heavy burden on the rest of the economy. On another level, there is direct competition for military and civilian shares of machine-building production. Here, the military share is apparently between one third and one half—not only is this much higher than the military share of general resources but also it is in direct conflict with civilian investment, the key to economic growth and production efficiency. The top level of competition is for the Soviet Union's R&D efforts and resources, which are of key importance to both sectors. The military share is usually estimated at, at least, one half. An important form of resource transfer from the military to the civilian sector would be the transfer of priority treatment, which is now almost exclusively granted to the military. This high-priority status encompasses all aspects of production, ranging from first priority in the supply of quality inputs and inputs in short supply, to the right to disrupt and preempt civilian production in order to provide for military needs, to direct administrative connections to top officials to clear away any problem or obstacle. The priority granted to the military facilitates its operation, even under the generally adverse conditions of central planning. The civilian sector suffers twice, once as a result of the system and a second time from the bottlenecks created by the system's priorities.

Priorities are enforced in two ways: first, by granting the military direct control over inputs and facilities (such as the nine military machine-building ministries), and, second, by granting the military the right to preempt civilian operations whenever needed. This second right is especially valuable, because the military can impose R&D activities on civilian institutions (such as the Academy of Sciences), and because it enables the military to skim off the best-quality products from civilian manufacturers, usually at regular prices. The most critical victims of the military's priority are the quality of civilian producer goods, especially machinery, and, even worse, the level and quality of civilian R&D activity. Both were key elements in past failures and reform aspirations. The opportunities lost by the civilian sector to military priorities are very significant. In most cases there are no actual charges or payments for priorities but these real opportunity costs should be added to any estimate of the military burden.

When we turn to the question of the possible transfer of resources from the military to the civilian sector, a different scale applies. Although such resource transfer is always significant, its contribution to the civilian sector and to the reform rises as we move from general resources (such as manpower, energy, and construction capabilities) to machinery and equipment and to R&D resources, the weakest link of the system.

The transfer of priorities is even more important. Some steps to shift priority treatment from the military to the most important civilian efforts, like the machinery modernization drive, have been recently taken: A civilian machine-building ministry was closed down, and its tasks were transferred to a military ministry; elsewhere, specific civilian machine-building tasks were imposed on military ministries. These steps were accompanied by a barrage of admonitions against the poor quality of civilian machinery. This method may produce some positive results in the short run, as better equipment, R&D, managerial personnel, and supply lines become available. But cardinal changes in designs, in equipment, and in materials cannot be made overnight. Priority shifting is clearly not a long-term solution, unless military capacities are transferred permanently to the civilian sector and to the reform environment.

Priority treatment conducted by the existing methods directly contradicts the entire concept of reform, and its continuation will definitely disrupt its advance. The preferred policy should be to phase out the administrative priority system and replace it with a Western-style industrial policy. A combination of regulations and economic leverages should be reemployed by the government to direct the allocation of some investment funds and R&D resources to national priority projects, as in Japan, for example.

It is very likely that, even with its somewhat reduced status, the military sector will be able to retain, at least for the medium term, most of its priority privileges. It will continue to operate as a centrally directed state sector, only partly integrating reforms. For much of the transition period, the civilian sector will benefit relatively little from transferred priorities and will be hurt by the priorities given to the military. The few civilian projects imposed on the military will have only a limited long-term impact.

Of special significance for the prospects of military transfer to the civilian sector is the intensity, timing, and shape of the planned military modernization program. The more intensive and the more closed this project is, the weaker the impact of the transfer will be in the civilian sector. An isolated effort will restrict the transfer of machinery, production capacity, and R&D. Most probably it will also deny the civilian sector any benefits from either a transfer of priorities or their elimination. The most favorable outcome for the civilian sector would be for military modernization to take place as a part of a larger economic reform in which there would be joint R&D and production facilities that would work simultaneously on civilian and military projects, with feedback and spillovers moving in both ways. Some of the leading technologies in both military and civilian sectors around the world are in the areas of electronics, information technology, and new materials development. In the long run, the optimal solution for both sectors and for the economy in general would likely result in a longer wait for military equipment and in extreme changes in the environment of secrecy and in the priority status of the military. The chances that this model, or at least a variant of it, will be implemented are somewhat higher because of the critical importance to the military of the R&D institutes of the National Academy of Sciences. The recently elevated status and enhanced freedom of the academy may also contribute to its success.

The more likely outcome is that a significant degree of isolation will prevail and that a very high proportion of quality machine-building and R&D capacity will be earmarked exclusively for military needs. The main thrust of the reform in the civilian sector might well be concentrated on the introduction of the new economic mechanisms of markets and competition. For R&D they will depend to a greater extent on the diffusion of second-line technologies and, to some extent, on imported technologies. The merging of the military sector into the economy will be postponed until the present phase of military modernization is completed.

Which model will be followed depends on the extent to which the military can be persuaded of the long-term benefits of transforming the Soviet economy. It also depends on the internal balance of political power, on the extent to which the leadership will manage to appoint its candidates to top military positions, and on the support the leadership receives from the military as distinct from other interest groups. Political and economic difficulties at home, and a less than complete external response, would steer the system away from the optimal path and into a compromise variant that would allow the military to proceed with most of its modernization plans as described above.

With this in mind, we can now turn back to the likely impact of the transfer of military resources to the civilian sector. Most of the existing models that try to make quantitative estimates avoid directly estimating the impact of particular transfers of resources or priorities. One exception is the estimation of the transfer of resources within the machine-building sector. Most of the existing models estimate that, beyond the very short term in which transfer is more difficult, the transfer ratio should be about one to one; that is, every ruble taken away from the military would add one ruble to the civilian sector. Although this is not a very surprising outcome, it is often a result of the underlying assumptions of the models and not an independently verified result.

Other models indicate that the transfer ratio is much less than one for one because, in a centrally planned system, military production enjoys a number of intrinsic advantages that are nontransferable to the civilian sector. These include the presence of outside competition, a very strong power on the demand side, and defining needs in technical, performance terms, rather than in efficiency terms. Nonetheless, most of the advantages enjoyed by the military have been determined by policy and are therefore potentially transferable.

Given a transfer of resources to a reformed civilian sector, one that is much more independent and driven by efficiency and profit motives, that sector should be able to take advantage of both the quantitative and the qualitative attributes of the transfer. This may not be entirely true in the beginning, during the transition period, when resources are still far from being optimally allocated, when the structure of incentives is incomplete, and when many infrastructure elements are still missing. On the other hand, on the basis of the preceding discussion on priorities and R&D and of additional work that is now under way, it can be strongly argued that, beyond the very short term, the transfer value of an average military ruble will be higher than one. Furthermore, a transfer ratio of one seems likely even during the transition period.

The next item that needs to be estimated is the expected decline of military spending. The best available estimates for past spending are those of the CIA which estimates that 4 to 5 percent annual real increase took place before 1975, dropping to merely 2 percent annual increases from 1976 to 1984, and climbing back to 3 percent after 1984 (a less certain estimate). It should be understood that these are real rates, calculated in relation to prices of each given year. To estimate the change in the burden of military spending on the economy, however, one has to account for the rate of increase in the cost of military spending relative to the general rise of prices in the economy. The reason for this is that the rise in military costs per unit of military output, in excess of the general price rise, reflects additional resources that have been transferred from civilian to military use. If, for example, the same number of equal-quality tanks had been produced in two consecutive years, but in the second year of production they required more labor, the constant price index would show no change in military production. But, because the tank cost more to produce the second year, more resources had to be transferred for military use.

Over the last decade or so, efforts to raise the quality of military equipment have resulted in cost overruns beyond any improvement in quality. Although the real rate of growth of military spending since 1976 was only slightly higher than the real rate of growth of the GNP, the share of military expenditures as a percentage of total GNP rose (according to CIA estimates) from 13 percent in 1975 to 15 to 17 percent in 1987. This was largely the result of an annual increase of about 3 percent in the relative prices of military products from 1976 to 1985. Any future military modernization program will be bound to generate relative cost increases, because the main efforts will be directed toward frontier technologies in which the Soviet Union is at a serious disadvantage.

It seems reasonable to concentrate on scenarios for changes in military spending involving cuts in the GNP share of defense. Any attempt to keep this share at its present level or to increase it significantly is likely to have negative economic consequences. A 1 percent annual increase in real defense expenditures, plus excess price increases, would likely result in a decline of the defense burden from, let's say, 17 percent of GNP today to 13 percent by the year 2000. A total freeze on defense expenditures together with zero price rises would bring the burden down to about 12 percent, still twice the current U.S. share. Judging from past behavior, these scenarios seem to be quite optimistic. A far more extreme assumption would be that the Soviet Union will aim to bring its own defense burden to a level equal that of the United States by the year 2005. In order to accomplish this, expenditures should decline at an annual rate of 4 percent, and relative prices should not rise at all. If prices should rise, real expenditures should decline even more. This seems beyond reasonable imagination.

Because the share of investment in GNP is expected to decline, or at least to remain stable, all the resources freed from defense will be transferred in the final account to consumption. For example, military machinery production capacity will be moved to produce civilian machinery and durable consumer goods, and civilian machinery production capacity will be transformed to produce consumer goods. The 1 percent military growth assumption would allow per capita consumption to increase over the transition period by an extra 0.3 percent per year. A total freeze would contribute an annual increment of 0.5 percent, and an extreme real cut would contribute an increment of about 1 percent per year. Even the lower rates would be quite significant additions to the basic rates projected for the rise in consumption levels. An extreme cut could accomplish, by itself, what the entire economy with no productivity growth could achieve. This could make a difference during the transitional period.

Finally, any real cut in the military budget would contribute to the solution of the state budget deficit problem, the number-one stumbling block to the continuation of the economic reform. However, because even the most optimistic scenario cannot envisage a normalization of the Soviet defense burden within the next fifteen years or so, it follows that our projections of future productivity gains may have been a little too high. The overestimate of efficiency growth may be still somewhat higher if we add the expected increased costs (and reduced efficiency) of a planned military modernization drive.

Economic Projections for the Future

The discussion so far has led to a number of conclusions about future Soviet economic growth and about the likelihood of successful modernization, which may lead to renew efforts to achieve military superiority. How realistic are the hypotheses about *perestroika* being a public relations smoke screen or about the Soviet Union's needing a breathing spell of a few years?

1. Our discussion has shown that, even if they were very successful, Soviet economic reforms at best would allow the Soviet Union to keep its relative economic position vis-à-vis the major Western powers. In any case, the absolute gaps between the Soviet Union and the NATO nations and between the entire socialist bloc and NATO will continue to increase for the near future. If one includes Japan and a few newly industrialized countries on the side of the West, or includes in it the entire OECD

group plus all of the above, then it becomes clear that the most the Soviet Union or the Soviet bloc can hope to achieve economically is to preserve its relative position. Indeed, a continuation of relative retreat is very plausible. It is also highly unlikely that the technological gap between the Soviet Union and the West will be closed over the projection period, either in the level of technologies used or in the ability to generate state-of-the-art technologies across a wide range of fields. It would be considered a great success if the Soviet Union were greatly to improve its ability to emulate, adapt, and diffuse existing Western technologies in a relatively short time.

2. The Soviet Union realizes that economic might is becoming an even more important element in the making of a world power than it has been in the past. This and the other arguments listed here most likely have shifted, or at least significantly tilted, Soviet priorities toward the goal of economic modernization.

3. Economic growth depends on reducing the military burden on resources, technology, and priorities. Even the most favorable assumptions cannot provide, within the next ten to fifteen years, or even beyond, enough economic growth to allow the Soviet Union to reduce its military burden to Western-sized shares (assuming that it will continue to aspire to parity, however defined). Indeed, the inability to reduce military spending to normal levels holds back the rate of economic growth. The military modernization program, if it is pursued intensively, will make things worse, as it will compete for the critical resources, capacity, and R&D in advanced technologies that are also needed for civilian modernization.

It is up to military experts to judge whether the military modernization program is viable in the short run and whether it can provide the Soviet Union with adequate military power during the transition period. Because the modernization program is being pushed ahead by the old methods of project-oriented priority, without waiting for economic reforms, and because the technologies involved are in the areas where the Soviet gap is the widest, it is questionable whether, even at the cost of great damage to the reform, this program can generate a qualitatively new level of military threat.

It follows that the Soviet Union can not proceed as it has before, and it can ill afford another costly bluff; the breathing spell theory must assume a very long spell in order to make sense. The Soviet Union may discover a way to proceed over the long term with a much higher military burden than its competitors, but the burden still will need to be significantly below its present level.

4. No one deludes himself that Western-style democracy is around the corner in the Soviet Union. But economic reform cannot succeed without additional reforms. It follows that any increase in the power of public opinion over the decision-making process is bound to make the government more attentive to consumption and welfare needs, and the government is going to find it increasingly difficult to justify putting aside the traditional allocations for the military, except under a clear threat from the outside.

5. The military establishment may not like reform at all. With the exception of a few military leaders who fully identify with the security interests of the Soviet Union (as distinct from its military interests), who agree with the new thinking (including the primacy of politics in international relations), and who are ready to accept a diminution of status, most soldiers will object. Most do not believe that politics or economics can provide security, that a country can trust its adversaries, that economic welfare should assume top priority, or even that economic reforms serve the long-term benefit of the military. Many in the military worry not only about status but also about their careers. Smaller armed forces mean not only fewer soldiers but also fewer generals. Although a reasonable modernization program may lure the support of some of the more educated young officers, it may also signal the end of the careers of many older officers with fewer technical skills.

It is difficult to determine Gorbachev's chances of success in imposing his will on the military. He has replaced a number of senior generals in key positions with younger men, and he has succeeded in distancing the military further from the Politburo, the center of decision making. He is engaged in an intensive propaganda campaign among the military, and he is most likely to tout the modernization program as an important military asset. Still, it is likely that, at a moment of crisis, the military would join a coalition opposing change.

6. Many factors and developments may keep the Soviet economy from proceeding along the most promising path. We expect the economy to develop at a somewhat slower than optimal rate and cannot rule out situations that might endanger Gorbachev's leadership. Western estimates of the performance of the Soviet economy during 1989 are grim. The Soviet population may be more patient than many seem to believe, but there must be a recognizable improvement in consumption levels, most importantly in foodstuffs, in the near future. Over the very short term, Gorbachev may have to depend more on the climate than on quick results of agricultural reform. A decision to cut investments and defense spending immediately also could provide short-term help.

Most observers agree that any attempt to revive the old economic system, even by reverting to the drastic means used by Stalin, is bound to fail. The false image of a fairly viable economy, which was projected to the outside world by the Soviet leadership under the old regime, has now withered away as a result of internal criticism and revelations. This does not completely exclude the possibility that such a change might be attempted. If Gorbachev falls, his replacement is likely to be someone who tries to revive Gorbachev's program, possibly in a more dynamic way. This person could well be Gorbachev himself, tiring at some point of too much muddling through and deciding to introduce a radical package of reforms.

7. The problem facing the West is whether to cooperate with the Soviet Union and, if so, how far. Such cooperation would help the Soviet Union by allowing it to reduce further its military burden and by facilitating aspects of economic reform. This no doubt would improve the performance of the Soviet economy to

a significant degree. It is true that Soviet economic successes could eventually be turned against the West in the form of a modernized military threat. It could be argued, even if the chances of this are small, why should the West help a hostile system? It is also true that the chances of war may become even greater if the Soviet Union fails in its attempted reforms. A failing power does not give up easily, and a renewed arms race in conjunction with economic difficulties could raise tensions to a dangerous level. Even the best-case scenario (from the Soviet point of view) does not point at present to a growing military threat or a substantial increase in relative economic power.

·4·
THE FATE OF THE NATIONALITIES
Paul A. Goble

STUDENTS OF SOVIET NATIONALITY problems increasingly resemble the blind men and the elephant. Those who focus on one part of the nationalities scene in the USSR are convinced that it will ultimately lead to a renewal of repression and the end of reform. Those who observe another are certain that it will result in a radical decentralization of power, possibly even the disintegration of the Soviet system. Those who consider still a third aspect are equally sure that it will not be an obstacle to reform and may even contribute to it. Like the observations of the blind men, each of these perspectives is based on apparently impressive evidence and captures an important truth; but equally like them, each view taken in isolation is a poor guide to the system as a whole and especially to the direction or directions in which it is heading.

Besides reflecting a longstanding tendency to consider nationality problems in isolation from other political issues, this fragmentation is a product of a dramatic change in Soviet reality. Thirty years ago, information about developments in the USSR was scanty and theories were elaborated to fill in the gaps. Now, under conditions of *glasnost,* we are so overwhelmed with information that we have neglected to develop theories to order this flood, preferring instead simply to report on the many interesting developments that the Soviet press offers for consideration. This approach has contributed to an almost Hegelian vertigo in which every development seems as likely as any other and in which the whole and the parts are often confused.

Nowhere is the need for the elaboration of theory greater than it is concerning Soviet nationality issues, precisely because of their extraordinary diversity. Unfortunately, no single obvious theory encompasses all of them. Before suggesting some of the elements of such a theory, three preliminary observations must be made:

1. The nationality scene is neither as complex nor as simple as is often supposed. Despite Soviet rhetoric about a country of more than one hundred national groups, the largest nationality forms 50 percent of the population, the three largest over 70 percent, and the twenty-two largest 97.4 percent. Moreover, the nationalities are divided both within and among themselves as to what they want and how they are prepared to go about getting it.

2. All Soviet citizens have multiple identities—ethnic, political, professional, and so on. Despite the claims of some nationalists, no one is simply an ethnic. Identities often compete with each other, a fact that the authorities have often used to good advantage. Just which identity will determine one's actions thus depends on circumstances.

3. Nationality affects virtually everything in the Soviet system; it is not, as is sometimes thought, confined to issues such as language and culture. Indeed, it may be far more important, if less obvious, in the economic and political spheres. But, while it affects everything, it determines relatively little, allowing both the authorities and the nationalities room to maneuver in achieving their goals.

Three Realities

For most of Soviet history, the nationalities question has been neglected by students of Soviet politics. The highly coercive system erected by Stalin seemed to preclude any active role for ethnic groups, and the extent to which the multinational composition of the population both undergirded and justified that coercion was seldom considered, either. Now that has changed. The dramatic upsurge of nationalist activism of various kinds under Gorbachev has led many in both the Soviet Union and the West to conclude that nationality problems are, if not the key, at least a central issue for the success of Gorbachev and the future of the USSR.

Judgments about the impact of nationality on the Soviet political system tend to divide into three main groups: One holds that nationalist activism will necessarily entail the reimposition of coercion, or at least the demise of Gorbachev's reform program. Another posits that ethnic activism may lead to or require a radical decentralization or even a disintegration of the system as it is now constituted. A third group argues that the impact of nationality on the system is overrated, that it can be dealt with in a series of relatively minor corrections.

Despite the certainty with which each of these three conclusions is often expressed, none of them is unambiguous or necessarily universal in its implications.

Given Russian history and the nature of Soviet political culture, suggestions that Moscow will ultimately and necessarily respond to the rising tide of ethnic assertiveness by returning to repression seem entirely credible. The options for repression range from regionally specific crackdowns to a broader return to Brezhnevism (without corruption) or even to Stalinism. Repression is not all or nothing, as even its proponents admit; rather, it can be given out in doses that may or may not have a broader, systemic impact. Consequently, repression is not so much an explanation as something that must be explained.

Nonetheless, it is possible to identify powerful arguments both for and against the use of repression in its many forms. One argument favoring repression of one kind or another is that a certain amount of tightening up would reassure the overwhelming majority of the population, which has not engaged in unrest. (It is often forgotten that nearly 90 percent of the demonstrators since Gorbachev came to power consist of members of nationalities that total fewer than 10 percent of the population.) Consequently, such a move might even be said to be popular. Repression also would tend to reaffirm the role of the party and of Moscow, at least for a short time. Given an essentially statist political culture, and given the fears of party officials that they are losing control, reaffirming the party's authority also would have significant support, at least in the short run. Finally, again in the short term, a certain amount of repression might help to increase workplace discipline, reducing economic dislocations brought on by both the reform and its uncertainty and thus increasing production briefly. That, too, would enjoy more support than one might think, particularly if economic problems were to continue to mount.

If the arguments and supporters of repression have a strong position, so does the other side. Any serious repression would antagonize the population further and undercut the possibilities for both domestic reform and foreign policy success. Consequently, reformers will oppose this out of principle, and many others will do so for prudential reasons. Second, because of the rise in popular expectations and the cultural and organizational changes that have already taken place since Gorbachev came to power, reimposition of repression except in isolated areas would be far more difficult and expensive than its maintenance would have been. Even the organs charged with public control are unlikely to want to tackle that, particularly since there are powerful reasons for thinking that such a course would not be sustainable. Third, a return to repression would represent an acknowledgment of the bankruptcy of the party's efforts at reform, thus undermining its authority still further, and would simply postpone dealing with many problems without offering any particular hope that they could be solved. While some conservatives may be prepared to live with a long slow slide, even most of them are unlikely to be willing to live with its implications. For this reason, even the conservatives are probably not nearly as enamoured of repression, at least on a general level, as is commonly supposed.

Nonetheless, if a policy of repression were adopted, it could be sustained for longer and with lower costs than many would like. By itself, it would not necessarily wreck the economy—it might even have some short-term positive effects—and it would certainly shore up the power if not the authority of those already in power. But, if the USSR is to compete in a postindustrial environment, it must confront both the need for a freer flow of information (something repression would constrict) and the need for a new basis for a social compact between rulers and ruled now that the bases of Marxism-Leninism are being undermined. Soviet patriotism undoubtedly remains strong, but it will weaken if the system cannot deliver, and that would both exacerbate and increase the importance of the very national feelings that the regime wants to contain.

A general return to repression also would have enormous implications for Soviet foreign policy. The basis of Soviet national security policy has been a continuing war scare, a sense of being surrounded by enemies, that has required both sacrifice and repression. Any general return to repression would almost certainly require a more aggressive foreign policy line and a larger investment in the military, which by itself would make the task of reviving the economy that much more difficult. Lesser amounts of repression, however, could contribute to stability in Soviet foreign policy. If Moscow is confident that it does not face serious domestic challenges—requiring the use of force as, for example, in the Caucasus and Central Asia—it may then be in a position to adopt a less threatening foreign posture and to engage in broader negotiations with the West. Here, too, the options are not all or nothing.

The second set of projections of the impact of nationality

points toward radical decentralization, or even disintegration, of the Soviet political system. These are two very different things. On the one hand, various kinds and degrees of decentralization each have their own implications for ethnic affairs. For example, economic decentralization to the republic level would have one set of consequences, while decentralization to industrial plant managers would have quite another. Furthermore, economic decentralization is a very different thing than cultural decentralization. Some decentralization efforts may be designed to spread responsibility and blame for things that go wrong, but all are based on an assumption that there are sufficient common interests, or force, to hold the system together and that devolution of power will in fact contribute to a strengthening of the system as a whole.

Disintegration, another matter altogether, would mean the exit, voluntary or otherwise, of one or more republics from the system. Such an exit could be either de jure or, less unlikely, de facto. This projection assumes that both commonality of interests and the ability to project force have broken down. Despite their dramatic quality, such projections are almost certainly wrong; in any case, there are only three republics—Estonia, Latvia, and Lithuania—in which sizeable groups are pushing for secession and in which the majority of the population could be mustered for such a step. Indeed, many republics even oppose decentralization, let alone disintegration, because this shift in responsibility would place burdens on them that they have not had to carry in the past and do not want to bear now. Consequently, the more likely projection is that of decentralization.

Powerful arguments and forces are pushing for significant decentralization. Such a step would help to increase efficiency if it did not go too far; thus, it would further the goals of political and economic reform. Furthermore, by shifting responsibility to the republics, decentralization would allow Moscow to avoid direct involvement in many issues that now must concern it. This would not only free Moscow's energies for other things but also, and importantly, it would limit the current tendency among many non-Russian groups to reduce all questions to the issue of us versus them. Finally, by indicating Moscow's tolerance of diversity, it would offer important foreign policy benefits by helping to transform Moscow's image not only in the West but also in the Third World.

At the same time, equally powerful forces are working against such steps. There are the longstanding Russian and Slavic fears (especially among the military) of disorder, the sense that transferring power to the periphery not only weakens the center but also threatens the entire system. Moreover, there is the very real possibility of copycat activism: Groups not now active might be tempted to pressure for more change both inside the USSR and in Eastern Europe. Because there is no certainty as to where all this might lead, conservatives are naturally sceptical of any change at all. Moreover, radical decentralization would have serious economic costs, especially if power were to descend primarily to the republics rather than to individual plants. In the absence of a true market, this would risk dividing the USSR into fifteen autarkic markets, something that could only undermine any possibility of getting the Soviet Union's economy moving again.

Neither radical decentralization nor disintegration appears to be sustainable for the long term. The Soviet Union is not Yugoslavia: It has a strong central state tradition and a dominant ethnic core—50 percent Russian and over 70 percent Slavic—that makes any kind of disintegration on nationality lines highly improbable. Indeed, if the three Baltic groups that most want independence were able to achieve it, they would likely find that they had set in motion forces that would prompt Moscow to reclaim its position, either de jure or de facto. And if the disintegration were more general, the Russian republic still would have disproportionate forces at its disposal. Most people who argue that disintegration is likely tend to forget that history would not end on the day that it took place.

Radical decentralization could pose many of the same challenges as disintegration, but, because it would be far less threatening to the center and its primary support groups, such a policy could be sustained at least temporarily. It would be particularly viable if it were confined to such secondary issues as culture (rather than economics) and if it were given to some regions rather than others, say the small Baltic republics (3 percent of the population) rather than to the Ukrainians (about 16 percent). Indeed, the simultaneous strengthening of center and periphery that Gorbachev talks about seems to be precisely this kind of balanced policy.

Quite obviously, disintegration would have important foreign policy consequences: It would create a radically destabilized situation on the Eurasian land mass, a bigger and more explosive Balkans. To say this is not to dismiss the moral claims of the peoples of the USSR—Russians included—for greater individual and collective rights, but rather to note that a disintegrated USSR would not necessarily be conducive to peace. Should such a process begin, it would require extraordinary care by outside powers lest it contribute to a disaster. But decentralization, too, poses important foreign policy challenges: Greater power for the Baltic republics to engage in foreign affairs would certainly have consequences for Western nonrecognition policy, and greater local authority elsewhere would give both Moscow and the republics a potentially more subtle mechanism for involvement in foreign trade and affairs. Whether the current round of reforms will go this far remains to be seen.

Finally, the third set of projections of nationality's impact suggest that Moscow can muddle through toward reform without directly addressing the role of nationality or making any fundamental changes in its status in Soviet society. Stated this badly, such a projection seems untenable, yet it appears to have been Gorbachev's own initial expectation, and it remains the unspoken assumption of many Soviet writers and Western observers. In a more moderate form, this projection holds that the Soviet system can cope with nationality by making only modest changes and that the suggestion that nationalities by themselves will transform or destroy the Soviet system is simply wrong.

As with the other two sets of projections, there are weighty arguments and forces pushing both for and against this one. First, despite the attention it has received, nationalist unrest and activism have not been as widespread or as serious as is sometimes claimed. Up to now, most of it has been confined to a fraction of the population of republics whose total population represents less than one tenth of the Soviet total. Perhaps more important, the demonstrations are not cumulative in their effects; they are not mutually supportive, and their goals often conflict, allowing the authorities to play one group against another. An obvious contrast is between the natives of the Baltics who want less Moscow investment and interference and the Central Asians who desperately need more of the former and are willing to tolerate some of the latter.

Second, Soviet loyalties have proved stronger and Soviet institutions more flexible and responsive than many in either Moscow or the West had assumed. While there has been much new ethnic assertiveness, it has not taken the form outside the Baltic states and Georgia of demands for independence. Indeed, precisely by allowing this activism, Moscow has demonstrated not the weakness of the Soviet state but its strength and flexibility. The Soviet leadership may even be able to use the unrest as a safety valve to prevent the formation of a larger and more serious challenge.

Third, popular activism often helps reformers to displace conservatives. That was clearly the case in the Baltic republics, where reformers actively sponsored the Peoples' Fronts in order to push out older leaders. The threat that unrest could be used either as an indictment against officials or as a measure of their progress provides Moscow with an important new means of controlling the periphery.

But, if the arguments for the muddling-through approach are strong, the arguments and especially the forces against it are at least equally impressive. Unrest on the periphery threatens the position of the party hierarchy and its ability to control the situation. In the past, republic leaders took their orders from Moscow and imposed them on the population. That allowed Moscow to rule the country indirectly and thus deflect much popular anger.

Now, that has changed: Republic leaders must increasingly reflect the views of their populations in order to mobilize them. That means, in turn, that they must increasingly represent their populations' interests against Moscow, leaving Moscow with fewer good options and more open to criticism from below.

Moreover, unrest on the periphery is clearly growing, inciting a Russian backlash. Russian political culture has traditionally shown little tolerance for dissent, has been generally afraid of instability, and often has had a maximalist approach to problems. Russians, who form the core of the Soviet state, are increasingly angry at what they perceive as too much permissiveness on the periphery. Many would respond with enthusiasm to any central leader who urged a crackdown, even if it ultimately meant that they would have to suffer greater restrictions themselves.

Perhaps the most potent argument of all against the muddling-through approach is the uncertainty of just where the current round of reforms will end, as far as the nationalities are concerned. Since Gorbachev came to power, virtually everything that has happened on the periphery has been the unintended consequence of reforms that sometimes allowed and sometimes provoked but never anticipated what happened. This pattern would be profoundly unsettling anywhere, but it is especially so in the Soviet Union. This fear and uncertainty affects more than just the Russian population and its party elite; it embraces large sections of virtually all non-Baltic nationalities. As a result, Gorbachev and the leadership are being forced to elaborate a more comprehensive nationality policy, something they had sought to avoid.

On balance then, this third set of projections of the impact of nationalities is not sustainable either, as Gorbachev himself explicitly acknowledged in his July 1, 1989, television address. There are simply too many pressures from too many directions to hold the line, and there is a sense that the pressures are increasing and even threatening public order. Moreover, the reformers need to do something that will either ward off or combine elements from the other two sets of projections, lest reform be restricted or killed by concerns over nationality.

Not surprisingly, attempts to muddle through would also have important foreign policy implications for Moscow and the rest of the world. Growing instability would certainly threaten any program to attract outside investment. Concerns that Moscow might slip into either broad-scale repression or disintegration would certainly compromise Gorbachev's attempts to portray the Soviet government as a reliable negotiating partner. Indeed, because many in the West, particularly in Western Europe and Scandinavia, are so sensitive to Moscow's handling of nationality issues, failure to contain national activism without killing reform may be as critical as anything Moscow can do. This is something that Soviet foreign minister Eduard Shevardnadze, an ethnic Georgian, certainly understands.

The Politics of Nationality

The temptation to choose one of these three sets of projections nonetheless remains very strong. Each viewed in isolation seems relatively credible, but, as we have seen, none appears to be sustainable at the systemic level for any length of time. Three conclusions suggest themselves:

1. To a remarkable extent, the three projections represent countervailing forces. Each one presupposes the existence of the others and to a certain extent is limited by it.

2. Despite their very different prognoses, all are based on an assessment of mostly common factors. This points the way toward the elaboration of a broader theory that would encompass all three.

3. All of them are closely related to but not integrated with the basic tension in Soviet politics today: the interaction between the need to maintain the political power of the elite and the desire to achieve significant economic expansion.

I want to suggest some of the ways in which these three projections can be combined and integrated into the broader issues of Soviet politics.

The maintenance of political power by the elite and the achievement of economic growth are to a large extent competitive. There is a choice between maintaining power now or achieving power worth having. The first view is generally held by conservatives and by members of the older generation, who are less concerned about the future. They want to hold onto power no matter what, and they are prepared to use coercion to do it. But, as the reformists have pointed out, that approach (which justifies stagnation) would reduce the Soviet Union to a Third-World level in certain respects by the year 2000.

The other view is generally held by reformers, who believe that their future power will be greater if they make certain kinds of concessions now. That is clearly Gorbachev's view and that of the rising generation. Whether he will succeed in anything like the short run remains to be seen. It is unlikely that the younger, self-confident group that shares these views can be kept out of the political equation for an entire generation. Moreover, even Soviet conservatives may ultimately support reforms out of deep-seated patriotism, if the choice of reform or decline is starkly put. This calculation may have been behind the initial support Gorbachev received from party conservatives, who honestly believed that something needed to be done but who now disagree with what the general secretary is doing.

The interaction of this tension between power and growth with nationality problems is interesting and complex. At the simplest level, it divides those who are more willing to risk reform, because they believe that Soviet identity is stronger and more vital than ethnic identity, from those who are not. But, at a deeper level, there is a fascinating interplay between support for repression or for decentralization, on the one hand, and commitment to political reform and economic growth, on the other.

These factors have important support groups and interact with each other. They can thus be seen as part of both a mental map of Soviet leaders and a diagram of political forces in Soviet society at large. Each not only interacts with, but also limits the others, at least at the extremes.

Let us consider each in turn. Too much repression would sacrifice decentralization, political reform, and economic growth, at least in the long term, while too little might have the same effect by destabilizing the situation, generating countervailing pressures for more repression, and killing off any chance for economic growth. The same holds true for decentralization. A radical program of decentralization would breed demands for more repression, hurt economic reform by creating autarkic regions or republics, and thus ultimately generate the countervailing forces that could kill political reform as well. Too much economic reform too quickly might also have analogous effects: It could threaten radical decentralization, thus hurting or killing the other three by generating countervailing forces. And a commitment to political reform, to the opening up of society, without attention to nationality issues, would do just the same thing.

In sum, each of these factors could limit, either directly or by generating countervailing forces, not only the other three but also itself, at least over the longer term. This suggests that they form a kind of parallelogram of Soviet power that is almost self-correcting and that could prevent the system from spinning out of control. This in turn suggests that the system will evolve gradually but not as quickly or as radically as anyone hopes or fears. Unfortunately, such conclusions are almost certainly far too optimistic. Differences in power between the backers of each of the factors are radically greater than such a scenario would require, and the opportunities for mistakes by participants are enormous. None of these factors is either/or, and change is not one process but rather is multifaceted. As we have seen, the possibilities for miscalculation are so large as to certainly happen.

Nonetheless, this correlation of unequal forces is likely to inform Soviet politics, particularly its approach to nationalities, over the longer term. As a result, developments on the Soviet periphery are unlikely to proceed as far and as fast as some hope and others fear. But by keeping this parallelogram in mind, we should be able at least to discern the true overall shape of the nationalities issue and thus guard against the facile assumption that today's headlines will be the next century's chapter titles.

What is all of this likely to mean over the next twenty or thirty years? Most likely, nationalities will present a complex and shifting kaleidoscopic pattern, in which the system will move both in whole and in part in the directions suggested by the projections listed above. These developments will likely take place both concomitantly and serially. At any one time, the four factors we have identified will likely have very different consequences and applications in different parts of the country. The Baltic republics, for example, may thus obtain virtual independence, while other areas may be subject to repression. Indeed, this possibility may have been the most important lesson Moscow has learned from the Gorbachev era so far: Actions taken one place do not necessarily require that similar actions be taken elsewhere. Over time, the system may lurch from reform to repression and then back again, with some forces now in eclipse and then reemerging. In short, Moscow may be under the Chinese curse of living in interesting times.

The future will be the product both of the existing pattern of forces and of human choices. The latter are virtually impossible to predict, but the former are known, and their impact is discoverable. These forces may be rearranged, and over time their shapes and role may be modified; it would be a tragedy if both the United States and the USSR forgot the lessons of the past and concluded that the future is unknowable and threatening, encouraging the very reaction that almost everyone now opposes.

·5·
PERESTROIKA AND THE SOVIET ARMY
John Erickson

WHAT ARE THE PROSPECTS of the Soviet armed forces for the 1990s? Ceasing to be the spoiled child of the Soviet government and the party is no new experience for the Soviet armed forces. The upheaval caused by the massive demobilization at the end of the civil war, the *voennaya reforma* (military reform) of the mid-1920s (a disguised purge), the struggles over motorization and mechanization, the murderous rampage visited by Stalin upon the Soviet high command, and Khrushchev's inroads into the professional military—all produced much wailing and gnashing of teeth within the Soviet officer corps. The military often has been obliged to adapt and bow to the party's perogatives.

The adaptability (or lack of it) of the Soviet military establishment and its role in the Soviet system is a matter of continuing importance, not least to the Soviet military itself, which is conscious of its position, perogatives, and requirements. It remains to be seen which of those features subsumed under the excitements of *perestroika* and *glasnost* are at once original and sustainable. After all, the battle cry of *perestroika* is by no means new for the

Soviet military: It was the banner headline for General Georgy Zhukov's article in the army's daily newspaper, *Krasnaya Zvezda,* in February 1941.

In addition to mistaking the Soviet military for a monolith, which it is not, Western commentary tends to mistake the relationship of the Soviet military to the party and the government for a zero-sum game. Nothing could be further from the truth, as even the most casual inspection of the past decade shows. Much of what is attributed to Mikhail Gorbachev owes its origins to that supposedly ideal environment for the military, the Leonid Brezhnev era. In spite of the sense of bloated and exaggerated military predominance, including Brezhnev's own inflated military reputation, the military was progressively tamed, and by one of its own, Marshal Ustinov. The beginning of the redistribution of place and prestige began as long ago as 1976, with the death of Marshal Grechko and the choice of Ustinov as defense minister. It was a good but incisive choice: Brezhnev was aware of the need to keep defense spending down, and Ustinov was prepared to do just that. Defense budget growth was held to 2 percent per annum after 1976. The great "investment debate" was about to unfold, extending well into the Gorbachev period.

At the same time, the military had to accustom itself to greater party intrusion into military affairs. What many Western analysts assumed to be the very acme of idyllic military-party relationships was simply not the case: A bloated military establishment did not please much of the military. Professional disgust and disdain can be quite a potent factor on both sides of the East-West divide.

While Brezhnev advertised himself most blatantly as the "outstanding military figure of the contemporary epoch," the military had to endure the steady intrusion of the party into military affairs. An exclusively defensive military doctrine was foisted upon the armed forces, generating a protracted investment debate which has not yet ceased. Even worse, arms control initiatives loomed that could only be realized at the cost of hitherto unthinkable limitations on Soviet offensive forces. More disquieting still was the appointment of Ogarkov as chief of the General Staff, the result of Ustinov's astute juggling, which shifted Kulikov to the Warsaw Pact in an apparent promotion yet subordinated him to Ogarkov. Ogarkov, in turn, reacted with violent polemics against Ustinov's budgetary constraints. Perhaps it was a matter not only of the budget but also of a military claim for more of a managerial role in the running of Soviet society, a step on the way to militarization, against which Brezhnev's successors steadily turned their faces—and rightly so.

The removal of Ogarkov, in 1984, was a signal that no blank check would be forthcoming for the military. Ogarkov's displacement and the subsequent downgrading of Grigory Romanov meant that Gorbachev would not be faced with a defense minister/defense industries manager in combination: Marshal Sergei Akhromeyev took over the General Staff and publicly adhered to the party line, while Sergei Sokolov slipped in unostentatiously— and bereft of Politburo rank—as defense minister. Gorbachev fell heir to all of this: to a military establishment now facing for the first time in a generation lack of direct representation on the Politburo, to an investment debate much intensified by the prospect of a vigorous American Strategic Defense Initiative (SDI) program, to the impact of rethinking and restructuring that preceded his appointment, to the advent of a new military generation, and to the presence of widening influences on the formulation of Soviet national security policy.

To revert to the terms of the zero-sum game for a moment, it cannot be said that the military has actually "lost" under Gorbachev, nor is it likely to do so. If anything, through a series of coincidences or convergences, deaths, accidents, and not a little design, the military establishment as a whole under Gorbachev has been brought back into line with a norm of army-party relations, with the military neither overly mighty nor totally subservient. The assertion, or reassertion, of the role of the party in military affairs is nothing new to the military; indeed, in its present form, this role is more acceptable because it portends a more reasonable approach to the crucial question of modernization. The demands of *perestroika*, much trumpeted abroad, do not yet foreshadow upheaval on a grand scale but rather pressure and persistence to introduce a smoothly running military machine.

Whatever the institutional configuration, the Politburo (even without its direct military representative) and the Soviet military will continue to share a joint stake in the viability and sustainability of Soviet military power. Gorbachev himself, as chairman of the all-powerful Defense Committee, has emphasized the immense importance of Soviet military cadres. Whatever the interservice divisions and rivalries, there seems to be a consensus that the long-term threat from the West is technological. The great debate, which will endure for some time, hangs on the question of how to pay for an appropriate Soviet response, raising in turn the issue of the focus of military development.

The military, in theory at least, has already adjusted to this reality: in a drastic revision of the "laws of war," the latest Soviet military version places political goals and economic strength in first priority, followed by scientific potential and morale/political strengths as the factors most vitally affecting the course and outcome of any future war. As the military has shifted its ground, the debate on Soviet national security policy has widened both in scope and in the diversity of its participants. It is true that the military monopoly in this area has now been broken, but it was in any event being eroded, if only because the military could not and would not be able to provide from its own resources all the expertise required to formulate valid judgments. Already, in 1984, the State Committee for Science and Technology of the USSR Council of Ministers had set up a special *nomenklatura* with expertise in the social, natural, and technical sciences bearing on military affairs and problems related to national security. There is as much, if not more, to be learned these days from such civilian publications as *Mashinstroenie* or Kiev's *Naukova Dumka* as there is from *Voenizdat.* Military strategy is beginning to be treated more broadly as a social science in its own right.

While none can deny the existence of the debate on national security and military policies, which has moved policy away from "absolute security" to "military sufficiency," a certain disquiet has emerged in the military over the intrusiveness of civilians and, even more important, the lack of boundaries for the debate. The outcome of the debate notwithstanding, it disposes completely of the idea that the Soviet military is a monolith, and indeed of the notion of a rigid military-civilian demarcation, although this is by no means a new phenomenon. All of this tends to suggest the emergence of a new type of Soviet "defense intellectual" and of a new "defense elite," along with pronounced politicization of military doctrine.

A clear picture must also take into account the effect of the personnel changes under Gorbachev, the progress of military modernization, and the internal consequences of the unilateral Soviet arms reductions, which are not quite what they seem. The Gorbachev changes have speeded up the rejuvenation of the aging Soviet high command. Retirements of significance began in the latter half of 1984, and accidents emptied more positions. The trend has been to accelerate the promotion of the more promising officers of the postwar generation. In the most senior echelons of the Soviet military leadership, Gorbachev has supervised or initiated ten changes, bringing in Dmitry Yazov as defense minister and replacing senior arms commanders such as Tolubko and S. G. Gorshkov with officers of the mold of Chernavin and Maksimov, who are more attuned to the "combined arms" approach, which predominates. Marshal Akhromeyev has left the General Staff and been replaced by General Mikhail Moiseyev, no doubt an appointment more to Yazov's taste but also undoubtedly affecting the prestige of the Soviet General Staff. The retirement of the hawkish Marshal Kulikov opens a vacancy within the Warsaw Pact command that may well no longer be accorded the distinction of a marshal's appointment and the status of a commander-in-chief designation.

Change within the regional commands has proceeded at a slightly more vigorous pace, as a number of military districts have been emptied out in order to man staff and command positions. Meanwhile the Afghan War veterans have not been ignored: Officers such as Slyusar, Kot, and Kuznetsov, representatives of an up-and-coming military generation with advanced ideas of its own, have intensified demands for the "smart" weapons Marshal Nikolai Ogarkov has repeatedly emphasized. Still, Soviet force modernization has not slowed, for all the rhetoric. New strategic offensive systems include solid-and liquid-propellant ICBMs and a new SSBN, together with projected long-range interceptors, air-defense ground lasers, an improved ASAT weapon; for the ground forces, new vehicles, antitank missiles, and attack helicopters; for the navy, a new generation of silent-running submarines and advanced electronics; and, not least—indeed, possibly by far the most important—computer-controlled satellite communications and a space-based weapon system.

With respect to Soviet arms control strategy, the military as an institution and the party in the person of Gorbachev seem to share a common view of parity with the United States. Under Brezhnev, it came to be recognized that parity was essentially cheaper than superiority. It is with this change, however, that the diminution of the status and the competence of the Soviet General Staff could become painfully clear, although the overall influence of the military as an institution must nevertheless remain crucial in the last resort. Certainly the military cannot fail to support elements of an arms control strategy if they contribute to predictability in the strategic environment, constrain the overall threat and facilitate its identity, lead to the denuclearization of NATO, and, above all, diminish if not actually eliminate the SDI threat. But does the military understand all of the implications?

The fundamental issue may be one of timing, with most of the military looking on political maneuvering as a means of gaining time, as opposed to relying on it to furnish security in its own right. (Like so many others, I have had interminable but not uninteresting or uninformed arguments with a broad spectrum of Soviet officers on this matter: It is clearly under debate.) At the same time, in addition to the external political benefits, some internal benefits can be construed for such unilateral moves as the most recent manpower and equipment reductions announced by Gorbachev.

Both *perestroika* and limited unilateralism in arms control have been used and are being used to implement essential rationalizations and to speed improvements in conventional forces. For example, the restructuring involving proposed reductions in manpower and equipment levels in the European theatre certainly preceded Gorbachev's initiatives. These reductions were born not so much of political idealism or altruism as of a growing recognition of the effectiveness of NATO's defensive firepower, the severe shortcomings in the structure of Soviet ground elements, the need to conduct defensive actions within the framework of offensive operations, and, above all, the need for a force structure capable of furnishing both mass and depth. Reductions of gross numbers, for all the political éclat and benefits for Soviet image building, substantially assist the streamlining of a cumbersome and unwieldy military machine without undue loss of operational effectiveness.[1] Rationalization of the system is long overdue, and in one other area, the Warsaw Pact, the move away from the army-division schema to an overall corps-brigade-battalion system could clearly improve effective integration of Soviet and non-Soviet forces: Non-Soviet forces could reorganize and reduce proportionately to Soviet reductions, leaving streamlined forces subject to selective modernization and capable of fleshing out an effective combat coalition.

Although the military cannot isolate itself from *perestroika,* by insisting upon and defending its special conditions the Soviet armed forces have managed to limit the process to some very necessary and much-publicized housecleaning, including that of the General Staff itself. This process does respond to criticism of Soviet military performance in Afghanistan and other military

---

[1]On November 10, 1987, at a presentation for the British 3rd Armoured Division, the Iron Division in Germany, I argued that a withdrawal of Soviet conventional forces in Europe would consist of six to seven divisions, with the possibility of two divisions from Central Group and two divisions from Southern Group also being moved out. However, restructuring along corps-brigade lines would not diminish capabilities, and ultimately nine Soviet corps would express parity with the NATO corps. This proposition received no demur when discussed with Soviet officers in Moscow in July 1988.

malpractices. But of much greater import is the relationship between the restructuring and the advent of major technological innovations. The Soviet military doubtless takes the view that military reorganization is a necessary step—whatever its coincidence with *perestroika*—toward setting up organizational frameworks to absorb the new technologies (provided they can be paid for). The structure of the armed forces and the scope of military development is likely to prove a very severe testing ground for the Soviet military, generating not only controversy, conflict, and competing claims within the military itself but also a fundamental divide as to whether this is a strictly military matter or one with significant political implications. In this context, the installation of Moiseyev at the Soviet General Staff takes on added significance: A relatively young officer, Moiseyev is by no means a military theorist, he is bereft of World War II experience, and he is a Far Easterner unconnected with any established military lobby save for his personal and professional association with Yazov.

The real test of the institutional place and power of the Soviet military will be perhaps not so much its involvement in budgetary adjustments but rather its the ability to manage in its own professional interests the relationship between a fundamental, far-reaching structural innovation and the associated weapons systems and technologies in the event of successful economic reform. The younger Soviet officers (and some of those not so young) perceive the inevitable necessity of a high-technology industrial base for space warfare. This recasts the question of the defense budget as a dilemma for politicians and military men alike: Can costly conventional capability be sustained in the face of massive R&D expenditure for space operations? (The secret 10-year Soviet space shuttle program cost a reputed $10 billion.)

This gives a somewhat different slant to Gorbachev's arms control strategy, including his unilateral restraints on existing Soviet conventional strengths, his attempt to engender multilateral cuts (primarily in Europe, and all as a cost-cutting exercise), and his apparent realization that the power relationships of the future will be based not on nuclear strength but on the utilization of space. It is more likely that the younger, technically trained officers will support this program of arms control, realizing its inherent advantages (as indeed I have indirect evidence that they do). The conservatives are not so much anti-*perestroika*, much less anti-Gorbachev, as simply unable to grasp the full implications of the grand design, which recognizes that radically new determinants of military power are almost at hand. It might well be that we are framing the wrong questions about not only the nature of the Soviet military but also the Soviet grand strategy. The Soviet revision of the laws of war and the revision of priorities in the correlation of forces are not, after all, remote academic abstractions.

The problem seems to be not so much that the military is losing ground under Gorbachev, as some would suggest by a simple institutional test (less public exposure, lack of full Politburo membership), but that it has yet to gain a new high ground by fundamentally reappraising the military requirements governing Soviet security, not merely for the present but reaching into the next century. The reassertion of party presence in military affairs is not necessarily to the gross disadvantage of the military as an institution, since the military has hardly been singled out, and certain norms have been reestablished and reaffirmed. The widening of the security debate, even if it does breach the military's monopoly on information (already a leaking sieve), is also not a net loss for the military. The joint civilian and military stake in Soviet military power remains, and there is a more politically sensitive realization that military security invests the Soviet regime with an element of legitimacy. If anything, the military can only gain over time with the broadened definition of "defense," even if it does link "national defense" with "state security," thus bringing about the greater involvement of the KGB and the party. Rather than focusing on the institutional rearrangement, which although it is significant is essentially transitional, we should be looking, as are a number of Soviet officers and defense intellectuals, for the implications of that structural change related to economic revitalization that will enable the Soviet Union to reenter the global competition in all sectors. Assuming a degree of success with economic reform, what will be the implications for Soviet external policies and the military's role within them?

The worst fears of the military (and other) conservatives—that the security of the Soviet Union will be gravely prejudiced, that the arms control strategy means a decline in Soviet capability in the military sphere—will not be realized in the coming decade. It can be assumed that Soviet military planners and political strategists envisage a competitive global environment, although not one that is inevitably confrontational. Indeed, recognition of such an environment is inherent in the argument that while the Soviet military will be, in the last resort, the arbiters of Soviet national security, military strength is no longer the sole measure of such security, nor is the application of military force in brute fashion a guarantor of success. On the contrary, Gorbachev's political initiatives and arms control proposals are themselves, attempts at a fundamental "systems shift" with the aim in the short-to-medium term of adjusting the "correlation of forces" more in the Soviet favor, or less to the Soviet disadvantage. What follows closely behind, if not actually in step, is the reorganization of the Soviet military system on functional lines, with the present restructuring marking only an interim phase or stage. The trick will be to bring these two attempts at "systems shift" into coherence and coincidence, and what links both is the acceptance of the priority of space competition. Space holds the promise of global presence, to be maintained and exploited for a variety of political, economic, and military purposes.

All this locks neatly into place, enhancing the role of the military, if it is assumed that the new Soviet military doctrine is not a mere deception (which it is not) and that there is a coherent connection between Gorbachev's arms control strategy—the proposed reduction in conventional capabilities, even unilaterally—and the need for resources to expand space-related R&D. Further, command in space negates nuclear power while at the same time enhancing conventional capabilities even as it qualitatively changes their nature. The trend to "negate" nuclear weapons in this fashion has its political counterpart in a strategy designed to render them irrelevant by sheer propagandistic and emotive demonstration. This is no simple deception or disinformation campaign, although elements of this are present; rather, it is a gigantic outflanking movement, an extremely high-risk strategy with as yet only a doubtful promise of payoff, one fraught with an ultimate peril for the West.

Whether it is palatable or not, the Soviet military has much to gain from the success of the Soviet arms control offensive, which even in the short term—by constraining the Western threat and inhibiting or hobbling Western technological advances in the military field—can give real substance to a defensive doctrine, facilitate rationalization and prudent reduction in the Soviet military establishment, and release resources for diversion to high-priority strategic tasks. Nonetheless, a form of military conservatism does now prevail, not least with respect to the problem of deterrence, to the maintenance of parity with the United States, and to a continuing commitment to evaluating the role of nuclear weapons beyond deterrence. Soviet military opinion seems to view the possibility of reductions in strategic arsenals as admissable, but given such reductions the greater will grow the imperative to maintain systems to defend against those weapons that survive, placing a premium on surprise. It is of little wonder, therefore, that the Soviet command has pressed for more money for aerospace defense, intelligence instruments, and the means to monitor American treaty compliances.

"Defensivism" looms large on the present Soviet military horizon and can be projected into the future, although it is not and will not be what is normally construed as "defense" in the West. The category of missions "vitally important" to the state and its survival includes defense against aerospace attack, neutralization of the opponent's military-economic potential, and destruction of enemy force concentrations. The implications are glaringly obvious and were already reflected in the adjustments to the laws of war made in 1984: Any future war will be dominated by high-tech weaponry capable of inflicting truly unacceptable (and possibly unimaginable) damage. This demands, therefore, a "systems shift" in alliance with *perestroika* that will specify vital missions and the reorganization required to accomplish them satisfactorily.

Thus, the overriding Soviet priority is to organize and ensure the resources for a deeply echeloned global defensive system with a major space-based component, an increasing emphasis on functional organization of Soviet military force (a pattern already established in the early 1980s though the unification of air defense resources), and an increasing emphasis on combined-arms capabilities exercised through unified commands. It is possible that such a shift, if put into full practice, will result in five major command/operational entities: a nuclear/strategic command, an aerospace strategic defense, an operational space command, general purpose forces, and logistics (rear services, mobilization, and reserves). This would reduce the separate service identities as operational elements, retaining them and their systems largely to train personnel in association with a diminishing number of military districts, a process already begun. The entire effort is designed to renew Soviet military power with respect to mobility, readiness, and surprise at all levels of conflict.

It can be argued that the Soviet military, while understanding the significance of and need for a global presence for specific defensive purposes, would not be averse to retrenchments facilitating the reallocation of resources to primary tasks. An international order, shaped increasingly by Soviet initiatives and responsive to Soviet priorities, with greater stability at less cost in blood (witness Afghanistan) and in money (witness Cuba) would not be inimical to Soviet military interests, assuming that "stability" means winning time to stave off the specter of strategic inferiority. Thus, attention will be paid to international duties, provided they are not too onerous and do not interfere with parrying American power, countering American prestige, and regulating the Sino-Soviet relationship and the neutralization of Europe that secures the Soviet western frontiers. All of this the military would accept under the banner of "war prevention," to its advantage.

In the course of a confidential East-West exchange in December 1988, I asked a Soviet officer whom I have known for many years for his estimate of the outcome of *perestroika*. The request elicited the following reply: Success would produce a major transformation of the system but would require time, outright failure would mean nothing less than neo-Stalinism, but the most disturbing facet of the situation is its uncertainty, which is clearly not conducive to a stable environment. This uncertainty will reach well into the next decade, and the intervening period will be larded with political risks in the USSR and beyond. The Soviet economist Leonid Abalkin has already pointed out that significant results will not appear before 1995, and this prolonged period of uncertainty will obviously intrude on the key task of implementing "reasonable sufficiency" and what is advertised as "defensive" doctrine. While much remains to be clarified, there seems to be general agreement that there can be no escape from a high-technology race. Defensive doctrine must adapt to the fundamentals of this arms race.

A high-risk aspect of Gorbachev's policy is that it hinges on the success of an arms control strategy that seeks to utilize the resources freed by reductions to stimulate a high-technology industrial base to meet the demands of an arms race in space, which demands rapid progress in information technology. Furthermore, a recent study of the "dynamic underwater warfare environment" expressly links "inner space" (the oceans) with space proper in a decidedly assertive concept of defensivism. The task is to block any American nuclear missile superiority and frustrate any American monopoly in space.

Recent Soviet discussion of mission structures, above all those of strategic missions, suggests that significant sections of the Soviet military are not persuaded of the eventual success of *perestroika* (or cannot afford to wait for it) and are engaged in setting out arguments and requirements which straddle *perestroika*'s success or failure. Although war prevention is advertised loudly as a move away from forces configured for war waging or war winning, Soviet military analysis in many instances is using the war-prevention device to suggest force levels and structures well fitted for war waging. While advancing the cause of deep cuts in nuclear forces, Gorbachev committed himself to maintaining strategic parity with the United States, yet for the Soviet military strategic parity means nuclear capability substantial enough to cause an opponent to think twice before launching a surprise nuclear strike and effective enough to blunt such an attack. Juggling with terms such as "stability" and "parity" does not eliminate the ambiguity inherent in "sufficiency."

Gorbachev's policies entail a double risk. The first, born of a strategy of arms control designed to reduce the threat of war combined with unilateral force restructuring intended to redistribute resources so as to compete in the new high-tech arms race, is the risk of polarizing the Soviet officer corps. This could have serious consequences in view of the second risky policy, the increasing political weight given to the KGB. But, if push comes to shove, and the military takes issue with liberalization and with "new thinking," then Gorbachev may have to lean more heavily on the military if he should doubt KGB support. This seems to be the crux of the military-KGB relationship, rather than any tendency toward military dictatorship or Bonapartism. One of the key factors will be the attitude of an officer corps that is increasingly distinguished by its educational attainments and scientific expertise, making it into a formidable lobby. Should a power struggle of some magnitude develop, which increasing internal strife and external frustrations might both precipitate and exacerbate, Gorbachev may well rediscover the indispensability of the military in a period of deepening uncertainty.

Gorbachev and his associates appear to anticipate a lengthy phase of adaptation and innovation in Soviet national security policies. But this alternative security scenario, which no longer relies on military strength alone, must nevertheless guarantee that it will not make the Soviet Union vulnerable to strategic surprise or consign the Soviet Union to strategic inferiority.

◆6◆

SOVIET GRAND STRATEGY: A NEW ERA?

Edward Luttwak

BG: Before Gorbachev

THE SOVIET UNION'S RELENTLESS ACCUMULATION of armed strength overshot its culminating point of success by the start of the 1970s. In perfect accordance with the paradoxical logic of strategy, more became less. Had Soviet weapon-making and force-raising proceeded at a more modest rate, and had the operational character of those forces not been so sharply offensive, Soviet military strength could still have provided ample security against all plausible threats while enhancing the Kremlin's diplomacy by reassuring friendly powers, influencing the nonaligned toward collaboration, and neutralizing adversaries.

As it was, the array of Soviet military forces became so threatening by the early 1970s, especially in conjunction with the Vietnam-caused military decline of the United States, that it evoked the vigilance of former friends, induced the nonaligned to cooperate with the Soviet Union's declared adversaries, and, above all,

149

persuaded the nonaligned to overcome their differences so as to combine against Moscow.

Strategy proved stronger than politics in country after country. The same defensive reaction drove Mao's ultraleftist regime into the arms of Nixon's United States, overcame both Gaullist and Socialist hesitations to strengthen French military ties with NATO, modified Sweden's implementation of its armed neutrality, and reshaped Third-World attitudes toward the Soviet Union's military presence in all its forms. Once seen in the Third World as a welcome counterweight to overwhelming Western strength, the visits of the Soviet navy, the flow of Soviet arms, and the growing numbers of Soviet military-technical advisers became suspect and themselves in need of counterweighting. More important, perceptions of a menacing Soviet Union turned the politics of most parties and most countries in the Western alliance in favor of higher defense budgets and "strong defense" attitudes. If conservative parties did not everywhere benefit at the voting booth, it was because their rivals to the left reacted to the same impulse in the same way. Social-democratic and socialist parties from Scandinavia to Iberia recast their policies on defense expenditure and alliance cooperation, and the British Labor party, which was pulled the other way by its peculiar internal dynamics, lost the ability to win general elections. In Italy, by contrast, even the Communist party adjusted, reversing its historic stance to endorse Italy's participation in the North Atlantic alliance.

The United States was not the first but rather almost the last member of NATO to experience these political dynamics. It was still experiencing post-Vietnam reductions (and recriminations) during the middle 1970s, when the rising profile of the Soviet threat was hardening attitudes and increasing defense budgets all over Europe. But of course the Reagan rearmament more than recouped the delay, in a belated but certainly not understated response to the relative increase in Soviet military power of the previous decade.

In theory, if the Soviet Union could have accelerated its military accumulation even more, it might have overtaken the reactions it provoked to reach an altogether higher curve of diplomatic suasion, with its own, farther removed, culminating point. Neutrals that until then had been stimulated into greater defensive efforts might have given up the task as hopeless and obeyed the same logic in different form by seeking safety in Moscow's benevolence on the best terms they could get. Countries that until then had coalesced against the Soviet Union might have deemed even their combined strength insufficient and judged bilateral conciliation safer than multilateral resistance. Further, Third World countries that were formerly jealous of their newly won independence might have concluded that it was best to accept gracefully an unavoidable new domination.

In such harsh circumstances, the United States might have been left with only few allies, very hardy or very remote from the Soviet Union (or both), before an exceptional rearmament effort could have redressed the imbalance.

In theory, the Soviet Union might have achieved a clear enough superiority to prohibit this attempt; in practice, no such superiority was attainable in one narrow but crucial category: strategic nuclear forces. The Soviet Union could theoretically attain a fully reliable counterforce capability against U.S. ballistic missiles, long-range bombers, and ballistic-missile submarines by such heroic measures as nuclear barrages on large oceanic tracts to wreck the missile submarines, somewhat smaller barrages around bomber bases (to destroy alerted bombers after take off), and multiple reprogrammed strikes on more than one thousand missile silos. All of these eventualities were dutifully evaluated, but the strategic-nuclear balance could only have become sufficiently delicate to make counterforce planning realistic in the wake of huge, unilateral reductions on the U.S. side. Before ridiculing those who took a dubious danger seriously, it is worth recalling that one-sided reductions large enough to make the danger less improbable have been continually and vehemently advocated.

In practice, the growth of Soviet military efforts decelerated even before the end of the 1970s to a point at which it was increasing still but at a slower rate, in accurate reflection of Soviet economic conditions. Hence there was no escape from the adverse dynamics of the paradoxical logic, whereby Soviet military power became too great to be calmly accepted but not great enough to intimidate, and the result was the Soviet Union's diplomatic isolation.

The same adverse dynamics attend any growth of relative military strength, and the negative reaction of other powers has been accepted throughout history as part of its cost. But that cost is worth paying only if it can be offset by the benefits of military power, defensive or offensive. The former case implies a prior state of vulnerability or of dependence on others for protection—both conditions that scarcely applied to the Soviet Union in the 1970s. The latter implies the possibility of gains, by armed conquest or by diplomacy. As we have seen, the Soviet Union was not gaining diplomatically during the 1970s because of its increasing relative military power, but rather losing, and doing so in ways that were dramatically evident from the beginning of the 1970s.

Examples of this are the theatricals that attended the U.S./Chinese reconciliation, Anwar Sadat's expulsion of Soviet advisors in Egypt, and the pointed declarations of pro-Western solidarity by formally nonaligned states from western Africa to Singapore.

The possibly unrealistic hypothesis of a purposeful Soviet grand strategy therefore left only one explanation for the continuing military accumulation of the 1970s: Conquest. That explanation was at once bizarre (in modern, nuclear circumstances) and entirely prosaic. Conquest was consistent with the entire character of Soviet military preparations and with specific initiatives such as the establishment of strategic-theater, all-service, command headquarters remote from the well-secured Moscow area (in which the political leaders can count on party-controlled KGB and ministry of the interior combat forces to counterbalance army troops). These command posts have no peacetime administrative functions; those were instead left to the central institutions and to the military districts. The first of these strategic headquarters was established in 1978, for the Far East at Irkutsk, followed by others for the western region, at Kiev, and for the southern region, at Tashkent.

Below the apex of these strategic headquarters, five "theater military operations" commands were also established for the more detailed planning and control of large-scale operations. The significance of this new superstructure of strategic and operational headquarters was compounded by the reconstitution of organic "Front" and "Army" echelons during the 1970s with their own artillery divisions and brigades respectively. Each artillery division has almost half the artillery firepower of the entire British army. The nonnuclear firepower massed in these two echelons greatly enhanced the Soviet army's ability to carry out offensives on the largest scale without resorting to battlefield nuclear weapons for initial frontbreaking.

The increase in the number of divisions, from fewer than one hundred and fifty in the mid-1960s to almost two hundred by the early 1980s (together with their expansion and modernization), generally increased the Soviet army's ability to carry out both defensive and offensive operations. But the new structures above the division level, especially the artillery siege trains at "Army" and "Front" level, clearly had a more offensive character.

As suggestive as the shift in the army's operational character was the overall condition of the Soviet Union, in which very negative long-term demographic and economic prospects coincided with great military strength, and with solid evidence of enhanced operational competence (notably in the last-minute airlifted rescue of the Ethiopian regime). A dangerous combination of long-term political pessimism and short-term military optimism could reasonably be attributed to the Soviet leadership of the time. This, of course, is the classic motive for deliberate war, to redeem an unfavorable future with current strength.

Thus if one transcended the spirit of the times to admit the possibility of the outlandish idea, a Soviet attempt at conquest could even be anticipated, given the eagerness of Soviet intrusions in the Middle East and Africa. Finally, in December 1979 there was conquest in Afghanistan, started by an elegant *coup de main* well prepared by subversion and followed by an occupation always desultory and ultimately abandoned.

In the immediate aftermath of the invasion, I attempted to define—strictly as a theoretical exercise—what further conquests the Soviet Union might undertake in order to enhance its long-term security by using military options acquired at great cost and bound to be transitory. I assumed that: 1. Soviet military accumulation would in fact evoke the negating reaction later manifested, most notably, in the Reagan rearmament; 2. the relative decline of the Soviet economy would preclude an added effort to outpace that reaction; and 3. Soviet expansion would be subjectively defensive, as had been the case with most continental empires throughout history.

Such "defensive" expansion, aimed at securing vulnerable peripheries by shielding them with further conquests (which are apt, in turn, to need like protection), is no less threatening for being "defensive." Nonetheless, in the nuclear age, especially, it is significantly different from idealistic expansion, in the Nazi style for example: The purpose (more security at the margin) limits the range of acceptable methods and excludes those that entail high (nuclear) risks.

Under the fixed premise that the Kremlin would sanction neither the planned use of nuclear weapons nor any offensive at all likely to evoke a nuclear response on the battlefield, let alone retaliation on Soviet metropolitan areas, I excluded the possibility of Soviet expansion into Western Europe in search of political security (to suppress Western stimulation of East European dissatisfactions). That left sundry possibilities of expansion for strategic security, of which the most notable was aimed at China, or rather at its thinly inhabited western regions. The scant population of this region, moreover, is partly non-Han, and it might be forcibly separated to form a "Turkestan People's Republic" analogous to the Mongolian People's Republic previously detached from Beijing's rule. Finally, under the heading of expansion for regional security, Iran was examined as a possible target, again for a combined military/political operation featuring the "liberation" of non-Farsi nationalities.

In contrast to all such sinister speculations, it was frequently noted at the time that there was nothing Napoleonic about Leonid Brezhnev, who was by then in glaring decrepitude. His even more decrepit and far more short-lived successors were just as unlikely in the role of conquerors. In the age of highly organized bureaucracies, this was a curiously personalistic argument, and it was especially unpersuasive when applied to the greatest empire in all of human history, with its highly structured military and police organs. Quite unbounded by the limits of nationality, and lacking the natural stability that only uncontested legitimacy can confer, the multinational and highly militarized Soviet empire, has its own dynamics of expansion, propelled by the recurrent impulse to secure exposed peripheries by further conquest. Hence, the decrepitude of the highest leaders in the Kremlin gerontocracy was not at all reassuring: Energetic leadership was needed not for conquest but rather for the opposite purpose of stopping the empire's expansionist drive, as Augustus finally intervened to prohibit further Roman conquest in his time, and as did other emperors in their time.

In any case, such speculations were beyond the scope of military analysis. The analysis of concrete military phenomena can define the pieces on the board and what moves each piece can accomplish, but not how the chess game will be played. That depends on political decisions that may be prophesied, perhaps, but not reliably predicted nor even interpreted unambiguously after the fact. In the Soviet case, as it happened, there were no further moves after the knight's sally into Afghanistan.

In the meantime, by the late 1970s, the ever-diminishing validity of central planning, the exhaustion of low-cost inputs (surplus rural labor, easily recovered raw materials), and the increasing handicap imposed by information barriers on technological progress reduced both output growth rates and the true value of that output, which was increasingly antiquated or of low quality or both, by world standards. In a fairly primitive war economy, planners can readily allocate inputs to the small number of intermediate products (steel, concrete, etc.) needed to support the production of basics for civilians and of whatever items the military quartermasters choose to order. Such production may be inefficient, but it will not be useless, because of the permanent shortage of civilian basics and the built-in prioritization of the military want-list. But Soviet planners were decreasingly able to choose among the exploding number of intermediate products (e.g., the myriad of diverse polymers), especially in meeting civilian demand without market prices to guide them. Hence, in addition to production inefficiencies, an increasing proportion of what was produced was useless.

At the same time, the official ideology was rapidly losing its appeal, because there was no compensating reversion to police terror in the full Stalinist style, and there was certainly no charismatic leadership to take its place. The outcome of felt impoverishment (relative even to Eastern Europe) was not a redoubled effort to overcome backwardness but rather demoralization in all its forms, from alcoholism at the base, to pervasive corruption in the middle of the bureaucratic pyramid, to inertia at its apex. This, in turn, fed back into the workings of the economy by way of absenteeism, slackness, indifference to waste, widespread theft, and even forms of sabotage, further reducing growth rates and degrading the quality of goods and services. The interim results of this vicious circle, quite evident by the early 1980s, were the disaffection of the intelligentsia, the declining ability of the system to co-opt the young, and the spreading rejection of transnational Sovietization among non-Russian populations, many of whose relative size was rapidly increasing because of higher birth rates.

AG: The Gorbachev Regime and its Grand Strategy

By the time Gorbachev became its new ruler in March 1985, the Soviet Union presented the sharpest possible contrast between internal decay and formidable military strength. The outside world was becoming increasingly aware of the relative decline of the Soviet economy and of the prevalence of acute societal ills. It could also be anticipated that the military superstructure would eventually be degraded as well, although there was little evidence as yet of technological stagnation.

In the meantime, however, it was actual Soviet military strength that counted, not the system's dismal prospects in the long term. That strength was threatening enough, as we have seen, to make of the Soviet Union the first true world power in human history, a dubious distinction marked by the worldwide coalition against Moscow.

As Gorbachev and his advisers surveyed the world scene in 1985, they were confronted by the defensive hostility of every country in East Asia, except for North Korea, itself vigilant towards the Soviet Union; of every country in the Americas, except for Cuba and Nicaragua; of every country in Europe, except for their own Eastern European clients and Greece, itself still a NATO member; of every country in North Africa and the Middle East, except for Libya, South Yemen, and Syria; and of every country in sub-Saharan Africa, except for Angola, Congo, Ethiopia, and Madagascar.

Only in southeastern and southern Asia did the Soviet Union have a worthy share of allies, clients and friends in Vietnam/ Cambodia, Afghanistan, Laos, and India (and the last was very restrictive of Soviet influence). For the rest, almost every country of any real weight in every region of the world was allied to, aligned with, or otherwise cooperative with the United States, formally or not, overtly or tacitly.

To be sure, this diplomatically unfavorable situation was the inevitable obverse of a most favorable military position. Had the United States been much stronger and the Soviet Union much weaker, China would not have been under compulsion to cooperate with the United States against the Soviet Union, France would at least have kept its distance from NATO, and a host of other countries would have been much less willing to collaborate in security matters with the United States, even if they would not necessarily have edged closer to the Soviet Union.

As it was, the wall of anxious vigilance that surrounded the Soviet Union was of great consequence not only diplomatically but also economically, for it precluded the legal importation of advanced technical know-how and of capital, while also restricting trade in various ways. The Soviet Union's few genuine allies and more numerous clients, on the other hand, were of small value as sources of advanced technology and even less of capital, as well as being generally unsatisfactory as trading partners. Several clients, moreover, were costly dependents.

This would hardly have mattered if the Soviet Union could have exploited its preponderance in nonnuclear capabilities for large-scale continental warfare, the very factor that had caused its diplomatic and economic isolation. But the continued believability of U.S., British, French and Chinese nuclear deterrence meant that the Soviet Union was paying the diplomatic and economic cost of this capability without being able to receive the military benefit of further conquest. So long as this was true, further increases in Soviet military power would be futile and doubly costly, in resources and by way of the further reactions they would evoke.

We may invent for ourselves an imaginary dialogue between Gorbachev, newly installed as party general secretary, and the elderly chief of the General Staff:

G: Can NATO invade us?

CoGS: No, we would defeat invasion with powerful blows.

G: Can China invade us?

CoGS: Never!

G: Can we invade Western Europe, or China, or reach the Persian Gulf oilfields?

CoGS: No. The enemy would use nuclear weapons if we were to prevail in nonnuclear combat.

G: Would another three thousand tanks, two thousand artillery pieces, six hundred combat aircraft, or an aircraft carrier change that outcome?

CoGS: No. They would accelerate our nonnuclear success and therefore provoke an earlier nuclear response.

G: Would another two hundred ICBMs, or five more nuclear-missile submarines preclude the enemy's nuclear response?

CoGS: No. Even if we can destroy a somewhat larger proportion of their nuclear arsenals, their surviving nuclear weapons would still be ample for a nuclear response.

G: So why are you asking for another three thousand tanks, two thousand artillery pieces, six hundred combat aircraft, and an aircraft carrier? And why should we add two hundred ICBMs, or five nuclear-missile submarines?

In other words, while its cost remained constant at best, by 1985 the marginal military benefit of additional Soviet military accumulation was zero, because defensive purposes were exhausted, and offensive purposes could still not be accomplished. At the same time, further military accumulation would inflict further diplomatic costs by intensifying the world's suspicion of Soviet intentions and hence increasing its security reaction. Thus, by 1985, the combined military/diplomatic marginal return of further Soviet military accumulation was not zero but actually negative. Reductions of the Soviet Union's military effort could yield a positive marginal return (diplomatically), while also reducing resource costs.

From that conclusion Gorbachev, as our imaginary strategist-king, could construct an entire policy: First, determine the culminating point of success for Soviet military accumulation, the level beyond which any increase in relative military strength cannot add to the Soviet Union's safety from attack, and adds less by way of useful intimidation than it provokes by way of defensive reactions. Second, reduce the relative military power of the Soviet Union (or just its offensive dimensions) step by step, until reaching back to that culminating point. Third, collect the diplomatic benefits in the form of a more favorable climate for all transactions, including such economic ones as less restricted trade, wider legal access to advanced technology, and perhaps capital loans in due course as well.

Since the March 1985 rise to power of the real Gorbachev, the lifelong party man and not our imaginary strategist-king, the full span of an American presidency has passed as of this writing. Still, the worldwide defensive coalition against the Soviet Union persists almost intact, simply because Soviet military power, too, is almost intact. Perhaps the regime has not yet become ready to confront its opponents inside the party, among the military professionals, and possibly in the military industries as well; or perhaps Gorbachev has been sufficiently badly advised to believe that smiles, symbolic gestures, and a few selective moves (INF, Afghanistan) would do the trick, abetted by the reassuring impact of various inadvertent displays of incompetence (including Chernobyl, the Cessna in Red Square, and the Armenian earthquake shambles).

It does seem now that, although the regime is still struggling with the active opposition of neo-Stalinist imperialists in the party leadership (and of some imperially inclined nationalists as well), and is still facing the bureaucratic resistance of the professional military, it has nevertheless finally decided to adopt a grand strategy that absolutely requires a reduction in the Soviet military threat perceived by the outside world.

The New Soviet Strategy of Reassurance as a Western Problem

The great unknown at this time is just how great the military reductions will be that the new Soviet "strategy of reassurance" will require in order to achieve its goal. Predictably enough, Gorbachev's announcement of future Soviet troop reductions has elicited the opinion that "he is eliminating the Soviet threat."[1] Although it is usually more cautiously stated, that is an opinion now spreading far and wide in the West.

It is not uncommon in politics to anticipate favorable developments, in this case, anticipation would treat expressed Soviet intentions as if they were accomplished facts. Furthermore, excessive optimism about the Soviet Union in general is virtually automatic on the part of those in every Western country who choose to be politically positioned to the left of whatever happens to be the center.

But there is also an element of honest misapprehension in the matter. The fervid hopes aroused by Gorbachev's initiatives at home and abroad are obscuring the overall goal now pursued by the Kremlin, even though Gorbachev and his colleagues have been perfectly honest about explaining it in every possible venue. It is their declared aim to transform the Soviet Union into a (very) Great Power, or superpower if one prefers, as opposed to the sui generis phenomenon it has been so far.

It confuses many in the West that the change that the regime is promoting is indeed as revolutionary as Gorbachev claims, even as its intended end point is so completely prosaic, that is, a Soviet

---

[1] In his statement at the 1989 *Wehrkunde* conference.

Union that would act as any Great Power of history has, determined to secure its possessions, and eager for more if opportunities arise. This apparent non sequitur is resolved by a reality that Soviet spokesmen are increasingly ready to recognize and even denounce: Soviet conduct so far has not been the normal conduct of a normal Great Power. It has resembled, rather, the conduct of a Great Power at war, albeit without much actual fighting. This characterization was obliquely if inadvertently recognized by those who equated the interception of KAL 007 with that of the Iran Air airbus. The U.S. Navy was, of course, at war with Iran in the Persian Gulf, itself a war zone.

The Gorbachev regime intends, apparently, to abandon its war-in-peace pursuit of limitless military aggrandizement, and its influence-seeking almost anywhere, at almost any cost and by almost any means, to adopt instead the normal conduct of a normal Great Power, subject to normal domestic priorities and restrained by normal inhibitions. If the regime remains on course, the outcome will not, therefore, be the "end of the Soviet threat" but rather a Soviet Union that would call for normal diplomatic vigilance and the upkeep of a normal military balance, as opposed to the far more stringent precautions warranted in the past and only inadequately or intermittently assured (hence Cuba, Afghanistan, and Nicaragua). Certainly the structures of Western security, notably NATO, would still be needed, whatever happens to the Soviet Union. Short of outright dissolution, the USSR would still be inherently stronger than any European coalition that was not itself highly militarized—and, of course, it would still be a nuclear superpower.

Western security policies, however, must also contend with one short-term and one long-term interim condition, even if there is no deviation from the regime's present "strategy of reassurance." The first interim condition is the continuing reality of Soviet military power, the substance of which has not been diminished by Gorbachev's declarations. The second and longer-term interim condition is the instability inherent in the transformation now under way. At best, we are in for an uncomfortably long interlude of cohabitation with a less threatening but more unstable Soviet Union. The reform of a decrepit empire driven by a variety of lively nationalisms is a high-risk proposition, and because of the existence of nuclear weapons, if for no other reason, the entire world will participate in that risk.

·7·

CHINA AND THE SOVIET UNION: PROSPECTS FOR THE YEARS AHEAD

Arthur Waldron

HOW WILL CHINA AND THE USSR affect one another in the decade ahead? Mikhail Gorbachev's trip to Beijing in May of 1989 provided a good initial perspective on the question. Meticulously planned, and tagged early on as a major story by the world media, Gorbachev's visit was intended to mark a bold Soviet reentry into the international game of China relations, which had been dominated since 1971 by the United States. The calculations behind it were probably similar to those made by President Richard Nixon and Henry Kissinger some seventeen years earlier: China was an emerging superpower, full of economic and military potential and destined to play a key role in a new triangular balance of world power.

But Gorbachev's trip was no smooth replay of Nixon's media triumph. The American president's visit had been flawlessly executed and seemed to confirm the assumptions about China on which it had been based. Gorbachev's trip, by contrast, went wrong from the start, and the China it revealed was not an

164

emerging superpower but rather a nation becoming unstuck. Beijing was unable to orchestrate the reception that a Soviet leader deserved, and as Gorbachev departed the Chinese government found itself confronted by a popular uprising. The most memorable images transmitted by the state-of-the-art television equipment positioned to cover Gorbachev's visit showed not toasts to mutual friendship but rather Chinese troops killing unarmed civilians in the streets of Beijing.

The forces that exploded in the democracy movement had been gaining strength long before Gorbachev's arrival. But, as in Eastern Europe and in the USSR itself, in China the Soviet leader also played a catalyzing role. The democracy movement and the Tiananmen massacre that ended it, at least for the moment, marked turning points in the history of twentieth-century China. In their aftermath, most of the assumptions that had previously guided policy required reexamination.

"Normalization" had been the catchword of American China policy since the early 1970s. It had seemed time to put aside Cold War suspicions in favor of mutual interests, to move forward into a period of coexistence, cooperation, and even friendship. Fundamental to this approach was a belief that China had become stable and united in purpose. Walter Mondale phrased this American assessment well during a visit to Beijing in 1979: "It is to the advantage, and not to the disadvantage of other nations when any nation becomes stable and prosperous, able to keep the peace within its own borders, and strong enough not to invite aggression from without. We heartily hope for the progress of China, and so far as by peaceable and legitimate means we are able we will do our part toward furthering that progress." Tiananmen shattered these hopes, and problems that were earlier dismissed as unthinkable now crowd the horizon.

The whole manner in which other powers think about China must change. During the coming decade the problem for Washington and for Moscow will no longer be what it has seemed to be since the 1970s: namely, bringing a stable China into the international system. Rather, it will be to cope with the worldwide consequences of chronic instability in China.

The Economy

Nowhere is this reversal clearer than it is in the economic realm. The China that Gorbachev visited early in 1989 was considered by many, Soviet economists included, to be a pioneering example of how planned economies could be reformed and made productive. Since the death of Mao Zedong in 1976, the Chinese economy had been dramatically reconstructed. Land had been leased on long terms to peasants, markets and limited private enterprise had been introduced, and foreign trade had been liberalized. All of these changes were far in advance of anything then being done in Eastern Europe or the USSR.

Results had been striking: Agricultural output had grown at about 8 percent annually since 1979, more than double the yearly average of the previous two decades, while industrial output had increased at perhaps 14 percent per year since 1983. Total GNP between 1980 and 1986 had grown at an average of 10 percent per year, almost twice as fast as it had under Mao. But, by the time Gorbachev arrived, the economy was beginning to flag, and its failures were feeding popular unrest. After Tiananmen, economic collapse became a real possibility.

Even before the political crisis began, the economy flashed danger signals. In the countryside the immediate benefits of reform were nearly exhausted. Decollectivization, by means of the long-term land leases, had produced a dramatic one-time upswing in production, but since peasants did not actually own the land they had no incentive to make the long-term investments needed to keep productivity growing. Price reform had been similarly incomplete: Prices were freed for some agricultural commodities, but for others state procurement continued, and peasants sometimes were paid with promissory notes whose redemption was uncertain. Industrial reform was also incomplete. It had been relatively easy to divide an agricultural commune back into private plots, but unscrambling the omelet of a state-owned factory proved to be nearly impossible. Reform strengthened management and stressed profits, but it did not privatize even to the limited extent that long-term leases did in the country. A host of perverse incentives led managers and workers not to increase long-term production but rather to cooperate in raising bonuses and diverting industrial assets to their own uses. Real private enterprise was given only a lukewarm welcome.

Nor were foreign trade and investment unalloyed successes. Exports grew, from 5.6 percent of national income in 1978 to 13.9 percent in 1986; total trade was perhaps 30 percent of GNP on the eve of Tiananmen. Yet China did not overtake little Taiwan in trade volume. Furthermore, foreign trade's role was not entirely positive: Many imports, for example, were of finished goods and luxuries that China did not need and could not afford. Joint ventures, widely trumpeted as the cutting edge of China's economic growth, were by and large unsuccessful.

Much of China's apparent increase in prosperity during the 1980s was short-lived or illusory. Rather than carry out reforms that could create self-sustaining growth, China has chosen increasingly to rely on borrowing. Foreign debt has mushroomed: More than U.S. $30 billion is now officially acknowledged, and this minimum figure does not include debts rumored to have been contracted by Chinese entrepreneurs informally through Hong Kong, a potentially enormous sum.

Until June 1989, however, it was still possible to imagine that China would solve these problems with a bold breakthrough into a much freer and more genuinely market-oriented system. Had this developed, funds would have become available for further investment and debt service and to sustain the rising standard of living essential to internal peace. "Normalization" could have continued. But the crushing of the democracy movement has made this extremely unlikely. In the years ahead economic difficulties likely will compound and exacerbate China's other problems.

Balance of payment and debt problems likely will grow more severe. The value of the Chinese currency, the renminbi, is still artificially high, despite a drop from 1.55 to the U.S. dollar in 1979 to 4.72 today. Further drops in value seem inevitable, and these will make difficult the management of foreign debt, particularly the substantial portion of the debt that is commercial and payable in Japanese yen. The situation will worsen if the economic situation in Hong Kong, which today is a major hard-currency market for China, deteriorates, which seems likely.

Another problem is chronic inflation. The lack of fiscal and monetary discipline in China during the 1980s (total currency in circulation was 145 billion renminbi in 1987, compared to 53 billion in 1983) had by 1989 created inflation unofficially estimated at 40 percent in some areas. Runs on banks occurred, as depositors withdrew funds to buy hard assets. Inflation has abated since June, but only because massive government subsidies have been used to drive down certain prices.

Ultimately, the most pressing economic problems for China will be the same as those faced by the USSR and Eastern Europe: government insolvency and mass poverty. Modernizing Asian states such as Taiwan and South Korea have demonstrated that autocracy can foster rapid economic growth by making and enforcing difficult policy choices that may hurt in the short run but that succeed brilliantly when given time. It may be that the Chinese leadership will be able to learn from their experience and undertake fundamental economic reform even while keeping politics under tight control. However, it seems more likely that China will continue to fumble over economic policies and fail to grow as fast as her leaders and her people want. Knowledge of the prosperity of other Asians has already created a revolution of rising expectations among many Chinese, and this will cause increasing frustration unless the gap between China and her economically advanced neighbors can be narrowed. At the moment, it seems safe to assume that this gap will widen.

Politics

As China's economic problems find political expression, the challenge to the government that was so evident early in 1989 is certain to revive. The demonstrations and massacre were a turning point in China's development comparable in importance to May 4, 1919, when the first great student demonstration took place in Beijing. Like the events of May 4, those of 1989 mark a watershed not only in politics, but also in culture and society.

1919 saw the beginning of revolutionary faith in China; 1989 witnessed its extinction. The collective sense that Communist policies and Communist leadership were best for China which sustained the People's Republic for forty years has now evaporated. The party has lost its legitimacy, and politics have begun to resemble the "warlord" period of the 1910s and 1920s, when personal and factional rivalries were resolved by force and the threat of force.

As in that period, China now lacks any strong leadership. In the USSR and central Europe much of the recent change has come from above. Gorbachev may not know exactly where he is going, but he is energetic: He travels, he speaks to his people, and he argues with his parliament. China's government, by contrast, is virtually invisible, and the people as a result are uninformed and increasingly alienated. The real holders of power, aged figures such as Deng Xiaoping and Yang Shangkun, stay in the background, choosing to work through protégés installed in positions of nominal authority. These younger men lack the political constituencies and personal prestige they would need to survive the passing of their mentors. As long as the elders live, it may be possible to maintain this situation. But once they pass, a struggle for power will break out during which most of the figures who are now familiar will probably disappear.

The most important question facing analysts of China at present is how that political transition will be handled, given popular antigovernment sentiment. Will it be smooth and well executed?

Or will it be protracted, inconclusive, and even bloody? At the time of Gorbachev's visit it was still possible to imagine the first possibility: The leadership might seize the initiative, compromise with the demonstrators who filled the streets of the capital, and use the prestige thus won to hold the country and the administration together for the challenges ahead.

After Tiananmen, however, the second scenario has gained plausibility. The coming struggle for power will most likely be resolved within the armed forces and security services, and these are now deeply divided. The People's Liberation Army waited a long time before moving on the demonstrators in Tiananmen. Clearly many officers opposed the action beforehand, and now that it has turned out disastrously their feelings of vindication will be matched by the rigid defensiveness of the crackdown's authors. It seems reasonable to assume that many Chinese officers and soldiers are deeply (if privately) disillusioned with government policy and leadership, feeling that their duty is to protect China, not to kill their compatriots, and that the return to the policies of the 1950s that is now under way can lead only to more poverty for their country. June 4 showed that armed force was the *ultima ratio* of Chinese politics, but the Chinese army came out of Tiananmen more divided than ever before.

Disillusionment within the military is matched elsewhere in Chinese society. The profound dissatisfaction of China's urban population, its industrial workers, some of its peasants, its intelligentsia, and its minorities is absolutely clear. The uprising in May and June engulfed China's major and many of her smaller cities. Television focused on Beijing, but there were massive demonstrations across the whole map, from Shanghai to faraway Dunhuang in Gansu. Vast numbers of urban residents are bitterly unhappy with the government and ready to march again if circumstances permit. Leadership of a renewed popular movement will come, as it has in the past, from the intelligentsia and its allies within the government.

At present the Chinese government is using all of its formidable apparatus of surveillance and control to prevent new demonstrations. This effort will almost certainly fail. Mass demonstrations in China usually occur in response to a factional dispute within the government. Sooner or later someone in the deeply divided administration or military will attempt to mobilize the people, as the reformist faction did in May and June of 1989, and the government then will face some difficult choices.

One option will be to crush the demonstrations with force. Even though the United States and other Western countries would probably respond to a second Tiananmen by imposing sanctions on China similar to those now applied to South Africa, thus gravely damaging its economy, and even though Eastern Europe and the Soviet Union might join in these sanctions, China's leadership might be willing to pay that price to hold on to power. But a second Tiananmen would probably be disastrous internally as well. China's military is now a brittle weapon, and it is likely to shatter into warring factions if it is again used against the Chinese people.

Nonetheless, if the government does not crush renewed opposition, then it will certainly be overthrown. Demonstrations and strikes will spread, soldiers and police will mutiny, and regional authorities will turn against the center. The party will quickly lose control of events, and as in Poland and Czechoslovakia groups will appear espousing radical new ideas about the nation's future shape. Perhaps the most important consequence of the Tiananmen massacre has been the way it has radicalized and transformed the Chinese opposition. Like such predecessors as the May Fourth movement, the present dissident movement is scoring its greatest success by transforming the Chinese political debate. Even as recently as May of 1989, most Chinese dissidents were oriented toward socialism, believing and hoping that the party might lead the way to reform. Now, however, it is a commonplace among them that saving the country will require the elimination of the party.

Meanwhile, overseas a whole new network of dissent has arisen since the June massacre. It contains not only marginal dissidents but also many people of great prestige and authority, and it commands the allegiance of most Chinese studying or living abroad. Heartened by the success of the East Europeans, these dissenters increasingly define themselves as anti-Communist. Their ideas are well known and influential, and they seem far more likely than reformist communism to provide the rationale for future political change.

Chinese leaders understand this, and we may assume that some of them are looking for a middle way: a guided, if forcibly mediated, transition of power. Perhaps the most likely scenario, given the Chinese talent for such things, is an attempt at a coup d'état like the one that overthrew the Gang of Four in 1976. It would be a mistake to imagine that the transition this time will be as smooth as it was then. China's people are stronger now than they have been in forty years. In 1976 the coup was carried out by elite secret service units; the role of the people was simply to celebrate when the news was made public. The next time the people will be directly involved—workers on strike, students protesting—and the whole process will be consequently far more chaotic and perhaps less decisive.

So the odds are against a clean transformation in which a coup at the center would carry the whole country with it. China is large and diverse, with many centripetal forces. Real power seems likely to shift more and more to localities. At present, orthodox Communist policies are being enforced with increasing effectiveness, particularly in North China. But will it be possible to extend these to the south and southwest, which are far from the center and have benefited greatly from the open policy? Probably not.

The Military

A China divided along regional lines would present a real challenge to current China policy, both American and Soviet. Both countries have tended to value China above all for its geopolitical weight. In the 1950s the Soviet Union used its Chinese alliance against the West; in the 1970s the United States sought to redress the balance. Just as Moscow after the Korean War proved willing to deliver advanced military technology to China (including, under one plan, a sample atomic bomb), so Washington since the Nixon administration has valued a quasi-alliance with China and has moved to make advanced military technology available to Beijing. After Tiananmen, these policies lost their rationale.

As with economic and political problems, problems in the military sphere were evident even before the Tiananmen massacre. Technical factors have always limited Sino-Western military cooperation. The People's Liberation Army is the world's largest armed force, and supporting and equipping it is a major economic burden. Yet it is not a very effective military force. It did badly even against unarmed students, and many doubt that it could, in conventional warfare, win victory at an acceptable cost even over Vietnam or Taiwan, let alone more formidable adversaries such as the USSR, India, or Japan. But the PLA will not be modernized soon: Improved weapons and more up-to-date training are simply not available. Today's China-produced military equipment is serviceable, but it lags several generations behind that of world leaders. To close this gap without foreign assistance would be impossible, both technically and economically. Until Tiananmen, various Western countries were assisting with technology and training, although this aid was insufficient to meet China's needs. Western aid seems certain to be terminated now, and it is unlikely to revive unless the political situation improves dramatically.

China's efforts at military modernization will also be hampered by the lack of a coherent strategy. In the 1960s the country concentrated its resources on the nuclear program, achieving impressive results. Today there is no single goal comparable to creating a Chinese bomb. The PLA's mission potentially ranges from fighting the USSR to seizing the Spratly Islands, so no limited group of key technologies can be identified on strategic grounds. Furthermore, the Chinese military's many constituencies push for everything from People's War to Star Wars. They seem unlikely to agree on a single coherent program of military modernization.

The most important point about China's military today is that it has been irretrievably politicized. Over the next decade decisions about everything from command assignments to weapons procurement will be based not on China's possible role in the world, but rather on the PLA's possible role within China. There will be little scope for the sort of geopolitical cooperation of which Kissinger and maybe even Gorbachev dreamed. The most likely war for China is a civil war.

Foreign Relations

The instability since the Tiananmen massacre threatens more than China's internal tranquility. It has created a number of possibilities that could undermine the peace of Asia. Some sort of crisis involving Hong Kong now seems almost inevitable, nor can renewed tension with Taiwan be ruled out. These will naturally concern Japan. Over the longer term, if China does not manage to stabilize, problems in the borderlands could draw China into conflict with the USSR.

The Hong Kong problem is now very clear. Beijing has spelled out its unwillingness to allow democracy or genuine political dissent in the territory after it takes control in 1997. Economic conditions there are already deteriorating and, absent some improvement in Beijing, seem likely to continue to do so. If emigration accelerates and anti-Communist feeling continues to spread in the colony, it is quite conceivable that China will move to take effective control before 1997, either directly, with the PLA, or indirectly, by insisting that the current British administration serve as no more than a conduit for Chinese instructions. The latter course might be resisted by Great Britain, which would further complicate matters.

The collapse of Hong Kong would worsen China's economic situation and exacerbate regional tensions. It could even contribute to regional and factional struggle within China: One can imagine a competition to control the colony between forces based in neighboring Guandong and those directly controlled by Beijing.

The renewal of tension in the Taiwan strait is less certain. Over the last decade tension between the governments in Taibei and Beijing has relaxed to the greatest extent ever, and until recently it has been possible to envision continued improvement. Developments on both sides of the strait have now changed that. On the Taiwan side increased democratization has made the option of Taiwanese independence increasingly attractive. Beijing has contributed much to this situation, by working systematically to isolate Taiwan internationally. The increasing power and self-sufficiency of Taiwan's armed forces have made the possibility of independence credible while leading Beijing to feel that it must respond sooner rather than later. As the internal situation deteriorates in China, and particularly as the army becomes more divided, patriotic and nationalistic appeals will become politically attractive. This could lead to an attempt to force unification.

The post-Tiananmen international atmosphere, however, will greatly complicate such moves. Foreign countries no longer side with Beijing instinctively, and an attempt to assert control over Taiwan could conceivably lead to the opposite outcome. Faced with real danger in the area, not only the United States but also European and other powers, now even including Eastern Europe and perhaps even the USSR, would likely call for a pragmatic solution including de facto recognition of both Chinas and entry of Taiwan into the United Nations. This would defeat Beijing's consistent policy of forty years.

Such disorder would pose a challenge to Japan. The instability of the Asian mainland in the 1920s and 1930s was one of the factors that pushed Japan to shift its foreign policy from peaceful internationalism to a unilateral attempt to dominate its neighbors. The parallel with the present is not precise, but it is close enough to warrant concern.

Sino-Soviet Relations

Sino-Soviet relations after Tiananmen are quite uncertain. We can assume that the scenarios we are considering here were scarcely considered in Soviet planning for the Gorbachev visit. Like Washington, Moscow at the time was clearly betting that China would prove to be fundamentally stable. It is clear that China will confront the USSR with new problems in the coming decade.

Some of these will be ideological. If reform continues in the Soviet Union and Eastern Europe, and if it continues to be resisted in China, then the splintering of the former socialist bloc will become even more complete than it was during the Chinese Cultural Revolution of the late 1960s and early 1970s. Then, at least, all countries in the bloc paid lip service to the same socialist ideals. Now, however, Eastern Europe rejects those ideals and provides compelling examples of how Communist regimes can be abolished. The examples of Poland, Czechoslovakia, and Romania are far more subversive of China than anything the West, or even Hong Kong, has to offer, and we can expect Beijing to denounce them.

Economic as well as political factors will lead Eastern Europe and the Soviet Union to lower the priority they give to relations with China. The China of the 1990s will have very little to offer the USSR or Eastern Europe, as either an economic or a political partner. Successful Asian countries, by contrast, have the money, products, and expertise that the former socialist bloc needs. Perhaps Gorbachev or his successor will become the author of a new Soviet Asian policy, one that will stress closer economic cooperation with Japan, South Korea, Taiwan, Singapore, and Southeast Asia. With China, it will seek little more than to avoid serious problems.

These exist potentially in the border areas, where ethnic groups are often divided between two countries. Mongolia and Xinjiang, in particular, could become arenas for Sino-Soviet confrontation. Serious potential problems also exist in the ideological realm. If China comes to think of itself as the last bastion of true socialism, while the USSR continues to reform, then tension along their common border will be as great as tension between China and the West. Nonetheless, confrontation over territory or ideology will probably be avoided, because it is in neither country's interest. As the year 2000 approaches, both the USSR and China face overwhelming domestic problems that would only be exacerbated by mutual hostilities. Furthermore, neither wants to be perceived as dangerous or irresponsible by the rich and developed countries from which each hopes to receive economic assistance.

Conclusion

China, from Tiananmen to the year 2000, seems likely to pose some unexpected challenges to the USSR and the rest of the world. On the eve of Gorbachev's visit in May of 1989, it was possible to envision developments in China that would validate the rationale for much global policy in the 1970s and after, to envision a stable and strong China playing an increasingly important role in both regional and global affairs. Although some policy planners seem unwilling to face the fact, Tiananmen has made such a possibility very unlikely and has confronted the world with the question of managing the impact of disorder in China.

Even under favorable assumptions—that succession struggles in Beijing will not turn violent, and that the winners will be reformers and not orthodox Communists—it is unrealistic to expect China to regain much of the ground lost in 1989 until the mid-1990s at the earliest. Under less favorable assumptions, regional division and even civil war within China are quite conceivable. Certainly the tension between the masses and the government will not be easily resolved. Furthermore, even if the most favorable scenario turns out to be correct, and China gets back on the path of reform rapidly and peacefully, the overwhelming economic and social problems China faces will greatly limit its international and even regional role.

As these facts are accepted in the West, they will probably lead to modifications in the Asian policies of the United States and its allies that will lead them to pay less attention to China and more to China's more prosperous and increasingly powerful neighbors. The USSR also seems likely to follow this course eventually, just as Gorbachev attempted in May of 1989 to emulate Richard Nixon and Jimmy Carter. The result will be to make China feel even more isolated, and thus perhaps to accelerate, as the Gorbachev visit did, the pace of inevitable change within China.

•8•
LOOKING BACK, LOOKING FORWARD: CONCLUSIONS
Walter Laqueur

A WRITER IN *Kommunist* (11, 1989), the political-theoretical organ of the Communist party of the Soviet Union, noted that some four years earlier I had observed that radical political reforms were impossible in the Soviet Union in the short or medium term. He added that developments since then, in particular the resolutions of the last party conference, had decisively refuted such skeptical views. This was not exactly what I had written; I had, in fact, taken issue with certain Western writers who had argued that evolutionary change in the Soviet Union was *a priori* impossible. Nonetheless, it was close to my assessment of the prospects of Soviet politics in the near future.

The discussion boils down to one question: What is radical political reform? Between 1987 and 1990 the parameters of cultural freedom in the Soviet Union gradually expanded, and Moscow became the most interesting world capital.

But cultural ferment is not a synonym for radical change at least not in the short run. In October 1905, under great public pressure, the Czarist government gave the Russian people a constitution that brought a parliament into being in which various political parties, including the Bolsheviks, were represented. This was radical political reform, even though it did not last long. The present Soviet leadership does not want a political system in which nonsocialist parties have official standing. Jean-Jacques Rousseau believed that freedom might be possible in the absence of an opposition, but few political thinkers have agreed with him.

We have witnessed in the last three years some major steps away from dictatorship and toward greater liberty, but there is still a long road to traverse, and the end is not in sight. In view of the economic difficulties and the nationalist ferment in various parts of the country, demands have grown to discontinue democratic experiments and to restore strong leadership. But no road leads back to Stalinism, and even Stalin would no longer be able to make the workers work in 1990. Five or even ten years of neo-Brezhnevism are not unthinkable, but this would simply postpone the day of reckoning. Among wide sections of the population there is the fear of freedom, the belief that "we always needed a strong hand," be it czar or commissar. From Peter I to the emancipation of the serfs to Lenin, Russian history has been a history of reform (or revolution) imposed from above. All kind of things can be imposed, but it is not certain that political freedom is one of them; at most, perhaps, the ground can be prepared. A framework for democratic institutions can be established, but, unless it is grounded in sufficient political maturity among the people, it will not last.

The style of Russian politics for centuries has been authoritarian, and so has been to a large degree the mentality of rulers and ruled alike. This may change, but only as the result of a cultural revolution affecting wide sections of the population. Such revolutions have occurred, but they have always taken a long time to unfold. It is easy to replace one set of rulers with another; it is infinitely more difficult to eradicate the mentality of unfreedom, to inculcate a spirit of civic responsibility, initiative, tolerance, and willingness to compromise. These virtues were never high on the czarist or the Bolshevik political agenda.

The transition from a totalitarian regime to a democratic system, even a "guided democracy," is a period of enormous tensions and difficulties. One political class will oppose the trend in any case; as far ahead as they can see a strong leader will be needed, or at the very least a strong Politburo. Pluralism, it has recently been pointed out, is not part of the Russian vocabulary. It may be suited for other traditions and cultures, many believe, but it should not be imported into the Soviet Union. Furthermore, the reformers themselves are divided as to how to accomplish the transition. A minority believes that "immediate and full democracy" should be introduced. Sakharov was not oblivious to the difficulties involved; he has said that "we are embarking on the building of a new state from the roof down." Others maintain that the country is simply not ready for a political revolution of this kind. Never in history has there been a transition from a precommodity economy to a market economy under a democratic order. In France as in other countries it was created by absolutism.[1] In Germany and Italy the totalitarian regime was dismantled following total military defeat, but the Soviet Union emerged victorious from World War II. Hence the need (to follow the arguments of some of the reformers) for a lengthy interim period of authoritarianism, just as France needed a Napoleon to introduce the *Code Napoleon* on which the subsequent development of French democracy was based. The dilemma has been described with great candor by A. Migranyan:

When the masses are involved in finding solutions to serious questions they do so partly to their own detriment, relying on populist sentiments rather than on serious ideas. And so a reformer cannot count on the masses for success.[2]

---

[1]Dialogue between I. Klyamkin and A. Migranyan, *Literaturnaia Gazeta*, August 16, 1989. One could think of a few exceptions to this rule, but then the Soviet Union is neither Switzerland nor Iceland.
[2]Ibid.

If it is true, this pessimistic appraisal raises doubts about the prospects of political freedom in the Soviet Union. For, quite obviously, there are no guarantees that the authoritarian leaders will be reformers and closet liberals; their inspiration could equally be of a very different kind.

This does not mean that there is no future for greater political freedom in the Soviet Union beyond the relative liberty enjoyed under enlightened and well-meaning autocrats, and that even this is not guaranteed. It does mean that the process will take, in all probability, years if not generations and that, in all probability, there will be major setbacks. The Soviet Union, it should be recalled, consists not only of Russians. Free election in the present conditions might well mean the disintegration of the union. Mikhail Gorbachev, to paraphrase Winston Churchill, has not been appointed chief of the party and head of state to preside over the secession of the republics.

During 1989 the mood in Moscow radically changed. There was growing criticism of the reform movement from both left and right. *Perestroika,* it was said, had lacked a clear direction from the very beginning and, all things considered, little had been achieved over the last few years. Having been charged with excessive skepticism, I almost turned optimist, at least in comparison with the conventional wisdom of the day.

What did the critics expect? That in a few years there would be decisive, irreversible changes in Soviet politics, economics and society with a genuine multiparty system and a president democratically elected? Did they really expect that the fruits of radical reform would be harvested within a few years?

Miracles are for those who believe in them. The rest of us will have to recall that five years, or even a decade or two, are but fleeting moments in the annals of a nation. Impatience is a bad counselor in political forecasting. As Otto von Bismarck once said, we may put the clock ahead, but this does not mean that time will pass more quickly. History seldom repeats itself, but it could be true nonetheless that the Gorbachev era, like the revolution of 1905, will enter history as the dress rehearsal for the more radical changes at a later date.

There is a strong temptation, according to one's political convictions, either to belittle the importance of the changes that have taken place in recent years in the Soviet Union or, on the contrary, to exaggerate them.[3] It is easy to deride them, for there have been many false dawns in the recent history of the Soviet Union: in 1934–35, at the end of the Second World War, at the time of Stalin's death, and also on subsequent occasions. But the fact that far-reaching changes did not take place on previous occasions does not necessarily mean that they will never happen, that, alone among the worlds' countries, the Soviet Union is exempt from change.

It is the test for true expertise in the field of art history to know a forgery from the authentic work, it is the test for a physician's skill to provide a correct diagnosis concerning health or disease, and it is the test for competence in politics not to miss the indications of real change. Those who claim that nothing ever changes in a certain country may often be right; it calls to mind the apocryphal story of the British Foreign Office official who claimed that the rumors of war were always wrong. He was only twice mistaken in his lifetime, in 1914 and in 1939.

It is tempting to mistake promise for achievement, to assume that the success of the reforms, the basic transformation of the system, has already taken place or is just around the corner. It is encouraging that, at long last, some of the truth about the Soviet Union has been freely discussed inside the country. But many of its problems are deeply rooted; to discuss them openly is a precondition for change, but no more than a precondition. Many in the West have a deep-seated desire to witness the emergence of a new Soviet Union, prosperous and free, no longer a threat to any of

---

[3]According to a knowledgeable Soviet observer "euphoria and unrestrained optimism" have been more widespread among visiting American academics and senators than among their Soviet hosts. L. Goldin, *Vek dvatsaty i mir*, 9, 1989, p. 5.

its neighbors. It is tempting to belittle the obstacles ahead and the length of the road.

How profitable is it to speculate about the future of the Soviet Union, or about other countries? The ancients had firm views about excessive preoccupation with the future. Aeschylus wrote that "of the future you shall know when it has come, before that forget it." Cato is reported to have said that he wondered how one haruspex could keep from laughing when he saw another.[4] Yet the ancients also knew that all human activity, even the most primitive, is based on anticipation. Our work here deals with the intentions, the reactions, and also the follies (to the extent that they can be anticipated) of men and women, more specifically with the political, social, and economic trends likely to emerge in the Soviet Union in the years to come. We have addressed such centrifugal forces as the nationalist movements of non-Russians and the vital vested interests of those who wish to perpetuate of the status quo, such as the strongly entrenched bureaucracy. The contributors to this book agree that the changes that have taken place in the Soviet Union in recent years are important, that they were long overdue, and that they will not soon lead to a new equilibrium. The magnitude of the tasks facing the Soviet Union, and not only in the economic field, is such that full success in the near future seems virtually impossible. But total breakdown seems almost equally unlikely. That the Soviet Union will face major crises in various fields goes without saying, but not every crisis is fatal; crises are the natural stuff of which politics are made. True, for both Soviet citizens and the outside world to associate Soviet society with a state of crisis is a new experience. Soviet citizens have been told that their system, in contrast to others, was free of conflict. They now have to unlearn this and get accustomed to living with disorder, not only de facto (which has been the case, of course, for a long time) but also de jure. It frequently is argued that Soviet citizens have been accustomed for so long to having

---

[4]Reported by Cicero. Haruspices were the officials in ancient Rome who interpreted the will of the gods by inspecting the entrails of animals.

their rulers think for them that they may find it psychologically very difficult to live with uncertainties and without clear guidance. Hence the strength of the authoritarian faction—in the widest sense—inside the Soviet Union, and hence the fear of freedom and the possibility that a new authoritarianism may replace the old.

But there is a tendency to overrate the severity of the crises facing the Soviet Union, at least in the short term. Such mistakes are frequently committed at times of ferment and change: Certain trends pointing to rapid and perhaps even revolutionary change, and the observer tends to forget that there are usually retarding factors, hidden from view but nonetheless very powerful. Like a true Hegelian, he discovers the seed and mistakes it for the ripe fruit. Ruling classes seldom, if ever, voluntarily leave the political scene, unless they have wholly lost their self-confidence. The trends initially discerned may prevail in the end, but usually the unfolding of events will take much longer than originally expected, except perhaps at a time of acute, dramatic crisis, when the pulse of history quickens and virtually anything might happen. But our time is not one of these ages of cataclysm, comparable perhaps to the aftermath of World War I or to the early 1930s when, in the wake of the great depression, in some countries power was in the streets.

In trying to assess the prospects of a country or a political system, yet another circumstance frequently is overlooked: The system ought to be viewed in a wider context rather than in isolation. Whether the prospects are bright or dim is a relative statement. The decisive criterion is, of course: Compared to what?

Thus, statements about the future of the Soviet Union make sense only when viewed in the international context and compared with Europe, the Far East, the United States, and of course the Third World. Predictions about the imminent downfall of the Soviet Union and China are premature for a variety of reasons. The annals of mankind are full of examples of political and social systems that did not function well but nevertheless continued to exist. What happened in Eastern Europe in 1989 will not necessarily repeat itself in the same way in Russia and China.

That Communist ideology is no longer widely and intensely believed goes without saying, and it is equally true that the only alternative at present is a populist-nationalist doctrine quite unsuited for a multinational empire. This undermines the legitimacy of the regime and in the long run will cause either its radical transformation or its ruin. A great many examples in history tend to show that this process may last a long time.

Is the regime too rigid for reform, can it not bend, only break? The Soviet system is unique in some essential respects. Major totalitarian systems have been defeated in war, but they have not so far voluntarily transformed themselves. Nonetheless, totalitarianism is a relatively recent phenomenon, and the fact that transformation has not taken place in the past does not necessarily mean that it will not take place over time in the future. In some respects in the economic, social, and cultural spheres the Soviet system already has moved beyond totalitarianism. The political structures, to be sure, have been far more resistant to basic change; for this reason, it would be premature to regard all changes made since 1985 as irreversible. Freedoms that have been given can be taken away as long as they are not anchored in the system. Hopes for far-reaching democratic changes in the near future are almost certainly bound to be disappointed. History, as a leading Russian writer of the nineteenth century once noted, is not the Nevsky Prospect (Leningrad's main street, a straight thoroughfare). It is full of twists and turnings, and there are bound to be major obstacles and setbacks.

Russia is again on the move; we know what its rulers want to achieve and what social and economic improvements the peoples of the Soviet Union are praying for. But the winds are blowing in different directions, and even sophisticated gauges are of only limited use. Some trends can be measured, but others, for instance those affecting the mood of the country, cannot.

One example should suffice: The Soviet Union is the country

of revolution, of the break with the past par excellence, yet it carries heavier burdens of history than almost any other country. One of these is the demographic burden, frequently ignored in debates, yet in the long term probably more important than the statistics about industrial and agricultural output. The immediate human losses of World War I were about a million or slightly more. But between 1917 and 1922 as the result of the civil war the population of the country shrunk by twelve or thirteen million. These figures include not only those who lost their lives but also the émigrés as well as indirect population losses. This was followed by collectivization and the purges of the 1930s. The direct and indirect losses of collectivization seem to have been on the order of millions of lives. Millions more were shot in the purges or died in the camps of the great terror of the 1930s. As for the losses of the Second World War, Nikita Khrushchev once gave a figure of twenty million. Others provided higher estimates, including indirect losses. These figures tell only part of the story, for those who disappeared were often the most active and capable elements of society: the old elite in the civil war, the new elite in the terror, and the most productive peasants during collectivization.

When the history of predictions concerning the mission and the likely fate of Russia is written one day, it will be both instructive and amusing. On one side of the ledger will be the correct prognostications, both general and specific in character, for instance the predictions concerning the superpower status of Russia made in the middle of the nineteenth century, a time when there was not much reason for optimism. Alexis de Tocqueville was only the most famous of a whole flock of French and German writers who predicted this. Also writing in the middle of the nineteenth century, Alexander Herzen and others took the coming of the revolution for granted. Later on, around the turn of the century, came specific forecasts that the Bolshevik party, as Lenin envisaged it, would inevitably lead to the dictatorship not of the proletariat but of one tyrant, or at best of a very small group of people: Georgi Plekhanov and Leon Trotsky noted this well before 1914, Rosa Luxemburg and Bertrand Russell did so soon after the revolution.

On the other side of the ledger are the incorrect forecasts. For many years after the revolution it was predicted that Bolshevik power would collapse within the next few days. Trotsky was an astute observer in some respects, but he was quite mistaken in his assessment of Stalin and Stalinism, and he firmly believed in the 1930s that the Soviet Union would be defeated in a future war. Stalin probably was the subject of more miscalculations and mis-understands than any other leader in either West or East; because he introduced some Russian nationalist and traditional symbols, it was thought that the normalization (whatever this meant) was just around the corner.

Mistakes, however egregious, have not necessarily meant ob-scurity. It is difficult to think of any nineteenth-century thinker whose vision of the future of his country was further from reality than either the poet (and diplomat and chief censor) Fyodor Tyutchev or the writer Fyodor Dostoyevski, each with his Pansla-vist dreams, his fantasies about Western Russophobia, and the idea of Russia as the only reliable fortress against revolutionary Europe. Yet in the 1980s the political ideas of Tyutchev and Dostoyevski again became immensely popular among sections of the Russian intelligentsia. But the most obvious case of mistaken prediction is, of course, that of Lenin. There could be no greater distance than that between the society he envisaged and the one that eventually prevailed in his country. Nonetheless, sixty-five years after his death Lenin is more often invoked than ever before as a guru and prophet in the Soviet Union; no official speech, no ideological article is complete without at least a quotation or two from his works.

To write about the future of a country, a political system, or a society is always risky. It can be predicted with certainty that some unforeseen (and unforeseeable) development will take place that will affect the course of events in the Soviet Union in the years to come. Trends that seem unimportant today may prove within a decade to be of great consequence, and vice versa. Yet speculations about the future are no idle pastime. Edmund Burke once noted that one should never plan the future by the past, but he did not practice what he preached, and his track record as a prognostician was not bad. There is no other known way of discussing the future except by reference to the past and the present, although contrary to popular belief history does not repeat itself. This has been, broadly speaking, the approach of those involved in this collective effort.

Contributors

JOHN ERICKSON is professor of politics and director of defense studies at the University of Edinburgh. His books, *The Road to Stalingrad* and *The Road to Berlin*, are the recognized standard works on the Soviet Union in the Second World War.

PAUL A. GOBLE, author of *Soviet Nationality Problems under Gorbachev*, is currently deputy director of research at Radio Liberty. Until recently he was special assistant for Soviet nationalities in the U.S. Department of State's Bureau of Intelligence and Research. Prior to joining the department in 1983, he was a Soviet affairs analyst at the Central Intelligence Agency and the Foreign Broadcast Information Service. The views expressed in this essay are his own and do not necessarily reflect those of the department or the U.S. government.

WALTER LAQUEUR is chairman of the International Research Council at the Center for Strategic and International Studies (CSIS) in Washington, D.C., and director of the Institute of

191

Contemporary History in London. He is the author, most recently, of *The Long Road to Freedom: Russia and Glasnost.*

EDWARD N. LUTTWAK has served as consultant to the Immediate Office of the Secretary of Defense, the National Security Council, and the U.S. Department of State. Since receiving his Ph.D. from Johns Hopkins University, Dr. Luttwak has written eight books, including *Strategy: The Logic of War and Peace* and *On the Meaning of Victory.*

GUR OFER is a professor of economics at the Hebrew University of Jerusalem and a visiting fellow at the Brookings Institution in Washington, D.C., as well as at the Harriman Institute of Columbia University.

ARTHUR WALDRON earned both undergraduate and graduate degrees at Harvard University and is currently assistant professor of history and East Asian studies at Princeton University. He specializes in the cultural and military aspects of Chinese history. His book *The Great Wall of China: From History to Myth* was published this year by Cambridge University Press.

Index

193